IMAGES

of America

ST. HELENA

This view of Main Street is looking south from Adams Street in 1886. On the right are J. R. Kettlewell and Son Hardware Store, Kettlewell's Boots and Shoes, Frank Alexander's Dry Goods, and McGeorge's Millinery (all burned down in 1887), Harry Stoeppler's Barber Shop, C. Hoffman's Furniture and Undertaking, Bon Ton Millinery, the *Times* newspaper, Barry and Campbell Millinery, W. A. C. Smith Real Estate and Insurance, Harold Jeweler, and Behrns Grocery. (Courtesy of the Marcella Howell Rice Collection.)

ON THE COVER: Peter Campini (third from left) is shown in the 1930s with a picking crew in his Pratt Avenue vineyard, which extended south almost to Fulton Lane. (Courtesy of Ida Merla Porterfield.)

IMAGES
of America

ST. HELENA

The St. Helena Historical Society
with Mariam Hansen

ARCADIA
PUBLISHING

Published by Arcadia Publishing
Charleston, South Carolina

Library of Congress Control Number: 2009934875

For all general information contact Arcadia Publishing at:
Telephone 843-853-2070
Fax 843-853-0044
E-mail sales@arcadiapublishing.com
For customer service and orders:
Toll-Free 1-888-313-2665

Visit us on the Internet at www.arcadiapublishing.com

*In memory of Kathleen Maki Kernberger (1943–2008),
a Napa Valley historian who inspired us all.*

CONTENTS

ACKNOWLEDGMENTS

The St. Helena Historical Society was founded in 2002 by a group of local individuals to preserve, exhibit, interpret, and provide access to the history of the St. Helena area.

Most of the credit for compiling this book goes to lead historian, researcher, and writer Mariam Hovanesian Hansen, with assistance from Kim Suverkrop Farmer and Susanne Austin Salvestrin, and additional research help from Sarah Lane and Lynn Johnson Rice. Thanks are also extended to historical consultant Lin Weber and Robyn Brode Orsini for copyediting and proofreading.

We wish to particularly thank Dave Kernberger, owner of Historic Photos Publishers, who with his wife, Kathy, diligently collected thousands of Napa County photographs and allowed us to use some of them in this book. Thanks also go to the Napa County Historical Society for providing access to their extensive photograph collection.

The outpouring of community support is evident by the number of donors who provided photographs and information. They include Kay Bissonette, E. Kergan Bruck, Joe Callizo, Helen Paris Christianson, Diane Dillon, First Presbyterian Church of St. Helena, George and Elsie Wood St. Helena Public Library, Grace Episcopal Church, the Frank and Edith Harrison Trust, Carolyn Kelperis, Gail Morgan Lane, Edna "Babe" McCormick Learned, Richard Lemme, Bill and Barbara Lincoln, the Menegon family, Peter Molinari, the John C. Money family, Napa Valley Wine Library Association, Helen Heibel Nelson, Marie Mason Oliver, Harold Pagendarm, Sandra Learned Perry, Noelle French Peterson, Yolanda Pincus, Ida Merla Porterfield, Julie Ghiringhelli Rehe, Lynn and Jeep Rice, Robert Louis Stevenson Silverado Museum, Rafael Rodriguez, Mary Jane Rossi, St. Helena Catholic Church, St. Helena Fire Department, St. Supery Winery, Joanne Kirkpatrick Sales, the Salvestrin family, the Harold Smith Sr. family, Jack and Marcey Smith, Ken Taplin, James Thorsen, and United Methodist Church of St. Helena.

While photographs convey information that words cannot, short captions can only give historical highlights. Cross-references to people and buildings outside each chapter help to convey relationships. We have done our best to be accurate, but there is always more to discover. We welcome corrections, additions, and more details about the historical record presented here—and about so much that is not. Please send them to the St. Helena Historical Society through our Web site at www.shstory.org, or mail them to P.O. Box 87, St. Helena, CA 94574.

INTRODUCTION

The St. Helena area was home to the Wappo people, a Yukian-speaking group who were the area's earliest inhabitants. The local tribelet village was called Anakotanoma or Anakanoma and was located near where Sulphur Creek meets the Napa River.

The earliest white settlers in St. Helena were John York, who lived on what is now Dean York Lane, and David Hudson, whose house is still located at Beringer Winery.

Dr. Edward Turner Bale was a British surgeon who was appointed to General Vallejo's California forces. When he married Maria Ygnacia Soberanes, a niece of Vallejo's, he converted to Catholicism and became a Mexican citizen. This allowed him to receive a Mexican land grant in Napa Valley consisting of 17,962 acres. Bale and his wife moved to their home on Whitehall Lane in 1843, and their family grew to six children. After Bale died in 1849, his family began selling portions of their vast holdings. One such sale was recorded in 1854 when Henry Still and Charles Walters bought 126 acres from Señora Bale. Lots on the property, which lay on the west side of the county road from Sulphur Creek to the future Madrona Avenue, were given to anyone who would start a business. The area became known as Hot Springs Township.

The railroad came to town in 1868, providing an important shipping nexus for fruit, grain, and mining products. New arrivals began planting vineyards and making wine in the 1860s. The wine industry began to thrive, encouraging more immigrants and more vineyards.

There are two theories about how the town name was changed. One says it was after the local branch of the Sons of Temperance; another gives credit to Mount St. Helena, a prominent landmark to the north. On March 24, 1876, St. Helena was incorporated as a town, and by 1886, the population had grown to 1,800 people. People from many lands and walks of life continued to relocate here, all adding to the town's complex and diverse history.

From early on, St. Helena was the commercial center of upper Napa Valley, including settlements to the east on Howell Mountain, in Pope Valley, and the villages of Rutherford and Oakville to the south. To buy shoes, see a dentist or doctor, attend a lodge meeting, or hear a politician required a trip into town. Students from outlying areas went to high school in St. Helena after attending rural schools. Churchgoers rode into town on Sundays to attend services. Tourists arrived by train, to be met by stagecoaches transporting them to resorts, spas, and other vacation destinations. Local people worked hard, but they knew how to have fun, too, as evidenced by the many saloons and eateries in town, as well as the numerous parades, dances, and other well-attended activities.

Today, three blocks of St. Helena's downtown are listed as a National Historic District on the National Register of Historic Places. Efforts to preserve agricultural land have helped the town retain its rural charm. St. Helena is proud of its heritage; besides preserving many of its fine old buildings, it has not lost deep traditions of camaraderie and generosity. St. Helena continues to reflect its history as a small town that is also one of the great wine-growing capitals of the world.

The photographs in this book are mostly taken from the 1880s to the 1960s. It is hoped that their presentation according to theme—the making of wine, the merchants and stores downtown, locals having fun and movies being made, some of the people who lived here, some of the homes they built, the churches and schools they attended, and life in outlying areas—will convey the spirit of St. Helena as it used to be and clarify ties to the past that help to make St. Helena the vibrant, attractive place it is today.

The ancient inhabitants of the Napa Valley, the Wappo, numbered around 10,000 in 1831 before the Gold Rush throngs inundated California. Due to the disease and encroachment of settlers on their land, by 1908 the Napa Valley population of Native Americans was estimated to have fallen to 40 people. The language and legends of the Wappo were passed down orally from generation to generation. Wappo people were known for their devotion to family, and their motto was "respect for elders, honor the children." The infant carrying board shown here was usually made of dogwood, with the curved rod protecting the face. Master weavers made baskets so tightly woven they could hold water and be used for cooking. (Courtesy of the Ina McCormick Hart Collection.)

One

MAKING WINE

Charles Krug (1825–1892) is considered by many to be the father of the Napa Valley wine industry. He pushed the vintners of the valley to produce better quality wines. It was Krug who pioneered the planting of European stock rather than the previously common mission variety. With his leadership, the Napa Valley grew from a tiny farming community into one of the foremost producers of wine in the United States. (Courtesy of St. Supery Winery.)

Joseph Atkinson first arrived in California in 1849 and engaged in business in San Francisco for 30 years. Around 1882, he sold his business and moved to Rutherford, where he owned 154 acres, eventually planting 115 of them in vines. This photograph shows his home and vineyard, now St. Supery Winery. With partner Seneca Ewer, he established the Ewer and Atkinson Winery in 1885, now Beaulieu Vineyards. (Courtesy of Historic Photos Publishers.)

A foreman supervises pruning in a vineyard near St. Helena in the early 1900s. Fruit quality depended on proper pruning, and growers such as Hamilton Crabb, Charles Krug, and George Crane led the way in developing the best pruning practices. If too much fruit grew on the vine, called overcropping, the grapes became inferior. Vines were usually head-pruned, as shown in this photograph. (Courtesy of the Frank and Edith Harrison Trust.)

10

A farm wife brings lunch to her husband as he ploughs the vineyard with horsepower around 1916. The spacing of vines, usually 12 feet apart, was determined by the width of the plough. The first tractors were not used until the 1910s, and small farms did not adopt them until much later. Most vineyards in the early days were dry-farmed, or farmed without irrigation. (Courtesy of Historic Photos Publishers.)

Here the Korte family harvests grapes with the family home visible in the background. Clemens and Maria named their property Pine Ridge after the trees found there. All hands were at work when it came time to pick grapes. The Kortes had seven children for their crew: Bernard, Frances, Marie, John, Clemens "Clem," Joseph, and Theresa. (See also pages 91 and 126.) (Courtesy of the Korte Family Collection.)

Clemens Korte (left) and a friend pose with boxes of grapes. Clemens came to this country from Germany in 1891 and married Maria Santel in Cincinnati in 1892. The couple bought the ranch on Ehlers Lane in 1898. Clemens engaged in viticulture, raising grapes and making wine until 1932, when he died. He was a devoted member of the St. Helena Catholic Church. (Courtesy of the Korte Family Collection.)

Grasshopper Company, a contract picking crew of the early 1930s, takes a rest on Spring Mountain at La Perla, the name of the Lemme family's property. After most Chinese had departed from the valley, Italians did most of the fieldwork, forming crews that moved together to ranches and often sleeping in campsites nearby. Pictured, from left to right, are Carlo Zara, John Landini, Joe Penoli, Vincenzio Ghiringhelli, Lino Guiducci, Domingo "Mike" Callizo, Cheso Catalani, and Santiago "Jack" Callizo. (Courtesy of Joe Callizo.)

To the right, Ray Ghiringhelli (see also page 67) is picking grapes in 1946 at the family property on Vineyard Avenue. Below, Ray's cousin, Erma Quaglia, picks grapes in 1946. Ray's father, Pietro, came to this country in 1902 and operated a bakery in San Francisco. In 1908, he married Luisa Camesa. They bought their vineyard on Vineyard Avenue in 1923. Their land became the Verde Vista housing tract in 1955. St. Helena's Italian population went from 25 in 1870 to 1,017 in 1910. They brought with them grape-growing and wine-making traditions that were quickly assimilated into the Napa Valley. After working for others, many bought their own vineyards as they prospered. (Photographs courtesy of the Ghiringhelli-Rehe family.)

Erma Quaglia , a friend, Luigi Quaglia, Ray Ghiringhelli, and Enes Ghiringhelli bring in the harvest in 1946. Luigi was born in Italy and came to this country in 1921. He and Erma Ghiringhelli (a cousin of Ray Ghiringhelli's) were married in 1926. After Luigi worked at the C and H Sugar plant in Crockett for 20 years, the couple moved to their ranch in St. Helena, located on Spring Street. (Courtesy of the Ghiringhelli-Rehe family.)

Clemens Korte (standing) and son Clem (riding on the horse) are shown hauling grapes during the harvest of 1917. After Clemens's death in 1932, Clem managed the ranch until 1969, with the help of his brother, Joseph. Their winery was Bonded Winery No. 951. The Korte ranch is still known for its quality Zinfandel grapes. (Courtesy of the Korte Family Collection.)

David Molinari was among one of the first Italian-Swiss in town, arriving here in 1872. He married Josephine Cavalli in 1892 and settled on Mills Lane in 1899. His sons, David and Peter, continued to operate the vineyard and make wine at Bonded Winery No. 955 after their father's death. Peter was one of the founders of the Silverado Cooperative Prune Dryer. Above, from left to right, are Jack Weiler, Peter Molinari, Michael Heitz, Marilyn Molinari, Ruby Heitz Molinari (Peter's wife), Walter Heitz, and Fred Heitz. (Courtesy of the Peter Molinari family.)

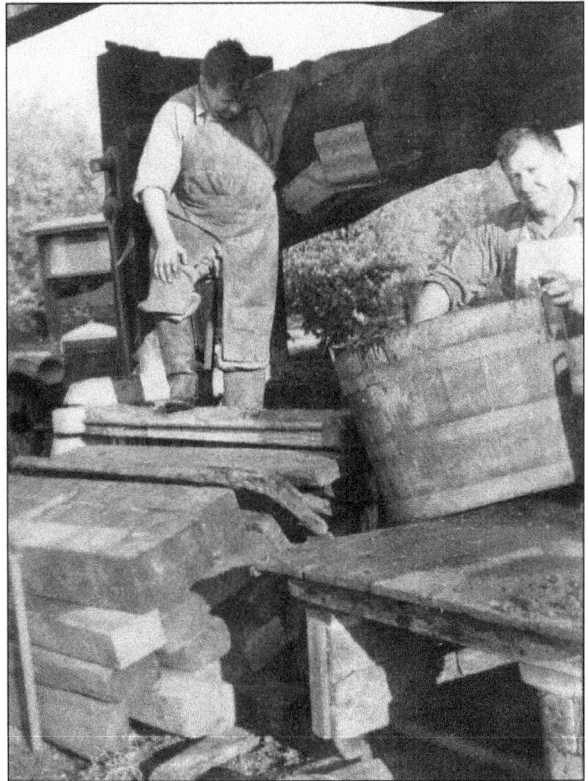

The Molinari family still lives at the farm and the Roman (beam) press, based on a Swiss design, is still there. The 30-foot log was felled on Spring Mountain. One end is attached to the hoisting equipment; the other end extends over the press, and the full weight of it presses the grapes. In the photograph at right are David (left) and Peter Molinari. (Courtesy of the Peter Molinari family.)

The Kortes made wine for their own use. Here they pose with their Roman press before Prohibition in 1920. Many families continued to produce wine during Prohibition, since the law allowed each household to make 200 gallons a year for home consumption. Clemens is shown in the photograph (standing, left) with his son, Clem (standing, right), and daughter, Marie (right), on the log. (Courtesy of the Korte Family Collection.)

Rafael Rodriguez and Joe Baranzini examine a grapevine at Inglenook Winery in Rutherford. The size of the crop from each vine was partly determined by the quantity of buds left after pruning was done during the winter. Rodriguez was vineyard manager at Inglenook Winery, continuing under the ownership of Francis Ford Coppola (as Niebaum-Coppola). Baranzini worked at both Inglenook Winery and Napanook Vineyard, having a longtime association with the Daniels family who owned both properties. (Courtesy of Rafael Rodriguez.)

Here is James McCord's Oak Grove Wine Cellar in 1900. James purchased land on Zinfandel Lane in 1855, and by 1877, he had 102 acres of grain, orchard, and vineyard. He built his winery in 1880 when he had 47 acres of vineyard. Production in 1882 was 60,000 gallons of wine and included such oddities as "Sparkling Burger." (Courtesy of Jack and Marcey Smith.)

The idea of building the impressive Greystone Winery was conceived in 1886 by William Bourn II, along with his partner, Everett Wise, as an answer to the Napa Valley vintners' debilitating reliance on the San Francisco wine merchants. It was constructed of volcanic stone from a local quarry and finished in the last months of 1889. Greystone was not only the largest winery in the world at the time, but also one of the first major winery cooperatives. (Courtesy of the George and Elsie Wood St. Helena Public Library.)

Fortune Chevalier (see also page 63) had a wholesale liquor business in San Francisco. He was prosperous enough to buy land near St. Helena in 1884 and built the stately Chateau Chevalier in 1891. Though it was later owned by the Grennans and the Harts, it was not until the Bissonettes acquired the business in 1969 that it became a functioning winery again, producing wine until 1984. (Courtesy of Kay Bissonette.)

The Trincheros purchased and revitalized the long dormant Sutter Home Winery (see also page 85) in 1947, shown here in 1951. The entire family was involved in the success of the fledgling business and would often work long hours. By 1951, the winery was producing over 50 types of wines. As a classic family winery, it sold about 65 percent of its wine out the front door. (Courtesy of the Napa Valley Wine Library Association.)

Two

DOWNTOWN

This photograph shows the view looking west on Hunt Avenue from Church Street in 1886. On the left are Heymann's Saloon, a barbershop, and Bussenius Drug Store. On the right are St. Helena Restaurant and Coffee Saloon, Mooney Brothers Grocery, and the Wonderful Drug Store. On Main Street, seen in the background, are the U.S. Post Office, Graf Jeweler, Carver National Bank, and the Windsor Hotel (see also page 94). (Courtesy of the Marcella Howell Rice Collection.)

In 1886, looking west on Spring Street, on the left are Europa House Saloon, owned by Antonio Forni (see also page 80) and Luigi Vasconi, and a bakery that burned down four years later. On the right are Harry Simmons's Saloon, which served St. Helena Brewery beer; Haar's Saloon; and the William Tell Hotel owned by Felix Salmina and Angelo Borla. (Courtesy of the Marcella Howell Rice Collection.)

This view looking north on Main Street from the corner of Spring Street in about 1900 remains recognizable today. Abraham Goodman opened his general store in 1879. On the left are the two buildings that originally housed the store: the corner building constructed in 1890 and the annex built in 1899 (today, Vintage Home and Ana's Cantina). Goodman's store still exists in the Richie Block up the street, now under different owners. (Courtesy of the Napa County Historical Society.)

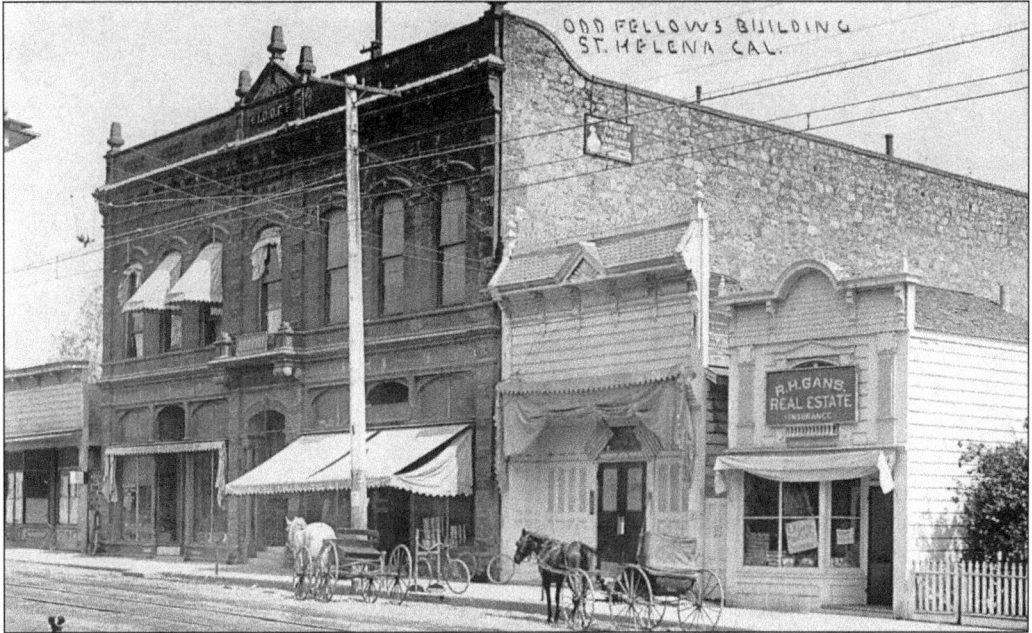

The Independent Order of Oddfellows building, on Main Street, was built in 1885. Upstairs were Dr. Sabin's dentist office, lodge rooms, and a large meeting room with excellent acoustics lit by three gas chandeliers. The white building to the right was the Elite Saloon, opened by Josef Reichert in 1886. He advertised cold Bavarian beer and fine wines. R. H. Gans opened a real estate office next door in 1904. This photograph was taken around 1910. (Courtesy of Historic Photos Publishers.)

Around 1910, this photograph looks south on Main Street from the corner of Pine Street. On the left (not shown) is Turnverein Hall (see also pages 40 and 105). On the right were the Galewsky home and the Fashion Livery Stable (Vanderbilt and Company today), belonging to Fred Mooney. The building with the bell tower was city hall from 1891 to 1955. A San Francisco, Vallejo, and Napa Valley Electric Railroad car is in the distance. (Courtesy of the Napa County Historical Society.)

21

The Americus Hose Company No. 2, formed in 1886, joined the ranks of St. Helena Hose No. 1 and St. Helena Hook and Ladder. Ben Bell (left) was elected fire chief of all three companies. The hose cart arrived on the train, nickel plated with 74-inch wheels. Harvey Lewelling (see also page 69) took this picture on Oak Avenue, which shows the wooden Catholic church and what is now the parochial school complex. (Courtesy of the St. Helena Fire Department.)

The St. Helena Livery Stable was located where the Sunshine Foods parking lot is today. Previous owners were Theron Ink, Samuel Kenyon, and Charles Gibbs. In this undated photograph, owner Irvin Wilson is the man on the left, standing in front of the carriage, which is probably taking passengers to Calistoga. In 1915, Wilson had kept up with progress and was operating a garage. (Courtesy of the George and Elsie Wood St. Helena Public Library.)

J. Rutledge Carriage and Sign Painter was first located next to the Palace Hotel on Main Street at Spring Street in 1881. Rutledge began painting houses and employed several assistants. Later he opened a paint store with a full line of paints and brushes. Charles Klubescheidt's sign is hanging below. Klubescheidt was "an excellent workman of house painting and decorative art." The family home still stands at 1445 Oak Avenue. (Courtesy of the George and Elsie Wood St. Helena Public Library.)

The stone jail near Tainter and Kearney Streets was constructed with thick walls in 1886 to keep obstreperous prisoners from annoying area residents with their loud and profane language. The lot was sold to the Catholic church, who demolished the jail in 1959 to build the new parish school (see page 93). (Courtesy of Jack and Marcey Smith.)

Jules E. Straus arrived in San Francisco in 1865. After working for Lazarus and Levy's general store, he started the J. E. Straus Express Store in 1870. In 1875, he moved to a new building at 1231 Main Street (shown here), where he had a flourishing business in dry goods. In 1881, he sold the store and left town. St. Helena Antiques occupies the building today. (Courtesy of the St. Helena Historical Society.)

The Windsor Hotel was opened by Sven Alstrom in 1881 (see also page 94). It contained three storefronts, a saloon, a dining room, and 28 rooms above. W. A. C. Smith (sign in center) had an accounting, banking, and insurance business, and he was the clerk of the St. Helena Water Company. (Courtesy of Gail Morgan Lane.)

This view of the west side of Main Street, south of Adams Street, was taken before 1900. The building on the left housed W. A. Mackinder Company—established in 1883 and "offering the most complete and reliable indemnity on acceptable risks"—and Wells Fargo and Company Express Agency. Joseph Kettlewell established a blacksmith shop in 1872 and built the white brick building seen on the right in 1889. His hardware store was on the ground floor, and doctors' offices were on the second floor. (Courtesy of the Clyde Kirkpatrick Collection.)

William T. Kibbler built this structure on Main Street in 1886. It is seen here as a hardware store decked out for July 4, around 1916. The first floor was a Safeway Store from 1928 to about 1950. In 1973, Dick Donaldson took over the Anderson Appliance store, changing the name to Donaldson's Appliance. The second floor was residential apartments for many years and is now Eagle and Rose Inn. (Courtesy of Historic Photos Publishers.)

This photograph shows a typical St. Helena saloon, with patrons taking a break from their labors. Saloon keepers tended to be first-generation immigrants and in 1876 included Germans Edward Heymann and August Stamer, Italians Louis Brunoni and Bernard Tosetti, and Irishman Garrett Fealey. By 1881, there were six watering holes that served as meeting places for men. (Courtesy of the Clyde Kirkpatrick Collection.)

In 1886, the U.S. Saloon, which also offered lodging and a bowling alley, was located at 1327 Railroad Avenue near Hunt Avenue. By 1899, it became the Roma Hotel, as seen in the photograph. The name had changed to the Miramonte Hotel by 1910. In 1922, the owner was Angelica Maliani. In 1947, Basilio Lucchesi owned the restaurant/hotel, and in 1993, Grant Showley took ownership, turning it into a restaurant. Today the structure is known as Cindy's Backstreet Kitchen. (Courtesy of the Frank and Edith Harrison Trust.)

Pearl Steam Laundry was situated between the Oddfellows building and Steves Hardware. It was founded between 1886 and 1899 and advertised for "white labor only." Martha Klubescheidt was one of the ironers. In 1900, Amneus and Gertsen were the owners, but by 1921 it was sold to Bernard Benitou and later to Tom Bradley. When Danny Kay bought the business around 1954, she changed the name to Danny Kay's Cleaners and moved the operation to Adams Street and Oak Avenue (now Napa Valley Coffee Roasting Company). (Above courtesy of St. Helena First Presbyterian Church; below courtesy of the St. Helena Historical Society.)

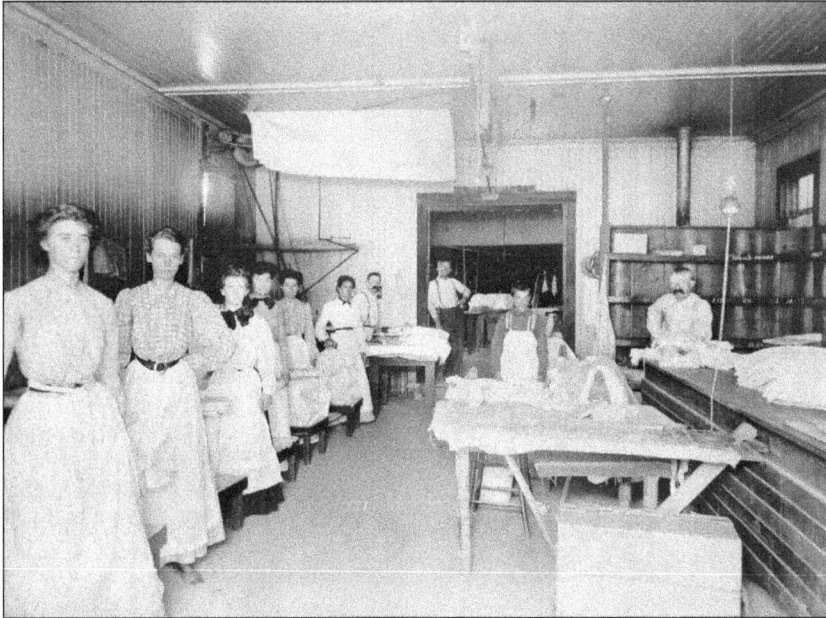

Elgin's Stable, founded in 1867 by William Elgin (see page 80), was located at 1156 Main Street, where St. Helena Cyclery is now. The *St. Helena Star* reported that "he has fine rigs, hires them at reasonable prices and keeps a first class livery stable." Elgin's son, Clarence, took over the stables in 1890. Later owners were Arthur and Ellery Murray, followed by Wallace Twichell. (Courtesy of the Clyde Kirkpatrick Collection.)

In 1891, this building was constructed on the corner of Main Street and Hunt Avenue for Daniel Otis Hunt, a prominent businessman. The Wonderful Drug Store of George A. Riggins was the first tenant; his initials and part of the store's name are embedded in the sidewalk. A pharmacy was located there for over 50 years, later becoming Brownlee's Drug Store, then Arighi Drug Company, followed by Vasconi's Pharmacy. On the second floor was the office of Dr. Alice Goetsch. (Courtesy of the Clyde Kirkpatrick Collection.)

The *St. Helena Star* was founded in September 1874, and the building shown here was built on Main Street in 1900. Above, from left to right in 1914, are Frank B. Mackinder (see also pages 43, 60, 70, and 85), Henry Laun, Orville Thompson, Louise Klubescheidt, and Theodore Simonson, taken when both the newspaper and the post office shared the same building. Mackinder was editor and owner of the *Star* (see also page 60) and was also postmaster from 1899 to 1915. Thompson began working at the post office in 1911 and became assistant postmaster. Klubescheidt, a St. Helena native, worked at the post office for 40 years. Simonson started working at the post office in 1900. Shown below, a crowd of men and boys mill about on a winter day around 1918. Note the office of J. G. Johnson on the right (see page 82). (Photographs courtesy of the St. Helena Historical Society.)

Inside the *St. Helena Star* plant, Augustine Fosetti, Louise Klubescheidt, and Edwin Paulson pose for the camera around 1913. Fosetti operated the linotype machine, later working in James Beard's print shop. Klubescheidt worked for the newspaper for a short time before starting at the post office. Paulson worked for the newspaper for 50 years and was named St. Helena Citizen of the Year in 1971. (Courtesy of the St. Helena Historical Society.)

The Post and Post Shoe Shop opened at 1228 Main Street in 1936 and was owned by Frank and Velma Post. Pictured here, Frank is seen working with his son and daughter. By 1942, Luke Paulich had taken over the business, renaming it St. Helena Shoe Re-Nuing. In 1967, Len Roman succeeded Luke and repaired shoes until 1992. Today Bellezza sells lingerie in the space. (Courtesy of St. Helena Historical Society.)

In the 1920s, the Windsor Hotel became the St. Helena Hotel, and the balcony was taken down (see also page 94). Beginning in the 1930s, records show successive ownership by Gruppo, Lewis, Lowman, Valentine, Sagadin, and Martin. Open for 128 years, the hotel is operated today by Mary Haney. Wright's Sweet Shoppe was a favorite spot for local children, selling ice cream and other goodies. Note the Indian Scout motorcycle and vintage cars parked in front of the shop. (Courtesy of the St. Helena Historical Society.)

Nicholas and Vasilia Paris, originally from Greece, owned a grocery store on Main Street from the early 1930s until Nicholas's death in 1945. The first location was in the building later known as Keller's Grocery (now a/k/a Bistro). The couple later moved the store across the street into a space in the Richie Block that now houses Goodman's Department Store. Nicholas is shown here among his wares. (Courtesy of Helen Paris Christianson.)

St. Gothard's Inn was built as a home in 1907 (see page 86) and converted to a hotel in 1911 by Herman Schultz, a Swiss, who named the inn after a place in his homeland. The popular hotel sat 50 people in the dining room. World War I diminished the travel business, and in 1921, the building became a hospital with 30 beds (see also page 76). In 1938, it again became a hotel and restaurant, with new, successive owners, Rose Pellegrini, John Domenici, and Arthur Treadwell. The hotel provided luxury lodging with a vineyard view. By 1963, the building became Grandview Apartments, which are still rented today. The photograph above shows the inn in the 1920s; the photograph below features the outside dining veranda. (Above photograph courtesy of the St. Helena Historical Society; below photograph courtesy of Jack and Marcey Smith.)

This 1922 photograph shows the west side of Main Street south of Adams Street, with Grant's Garage at left and the Oddfellows building at right. Philo Grant began his business as a bicycle repair shop, eventually adding automobile repair, the sale of gasoline, a new-car dealership, and an ambulance service. In 1927, Grant sold the business to Eddie Bonhote, who in turn sold the automobile repair shop to Phillip Thompson in 1945. Bonhote continued to repair bicycles. Since 1992, the building has been the home of Steves Hardware. (Courtesy of Historic Photos Publishers.)

A heavy snowstorm covered Main Street on January 15, 1932, and Frank Harrison was there to capture it from the west side of Main Street, north of Hunt Avenue. All power and telephones were out. Stores had to shovel snow off their sidewalks. Nearly every street in town was strewn with tree branches, and fallen trees blocked the highway. Children made snowmen downtown. (Courtesy of the Frank and Edith Harrison Trust.)

33

John Henry Steves (see also page 73) poses for a photographer in Steves Hardware in the 1940s. John started his business by doing plumbing and tinning. The store was located in the Oddfellows building from 1888 to 1992, before moving to the former Grant's Garage building next door. Warren Steves sold the business to Jerry Gard and Verino Menegon in 1955, after 77 years of family ownership. Menegon family members remain the present owners. (Courtesy of the Menegon family.)

Nelson and Margaret "Maggie" Outwaters opened the Gray Gables Hotel (see also pages 66 and 101) next to the Methodist church on Adams Street in 1898. With its broad verandas, friendly staff, and fine cuisine, it soon became a popular destination for locals and visitors alike. The hotel had 30 rooms in the main building plus cottages. Rates ranged from $2 per day to $12 per week. The hotel was sold to the Caricofs in 1907 and then to Mary Lorane. Upon Mary's death in 1944, it passed to Nicholas Taganas. Upon Nicholas's death in 1958, Margaret Mensch took over, but the hotel closed soon afterward. The building has been demolished and replaced with an office complex. (Courtesy of Historic Photos Publishers.)

The Napa Valley Railroad arrived in 1868; the first depot was located at Railroad and Hunt Avenues. By 1889, Southern Pacific Railroad had taken over and built a new station at Railroad Avenue and Pine Street, which is shown here. Southbound trains left twice a day (at 6:12 a.m. and 3:04 p.m.) for Vallejo and Oakland. Locals depended on regular train service for passengers until 1929, when buses became more popular. Freight trains continued until the 1980s. (Courtesy of Marie Mason Oliver.)

Early railroads were powered by steam and then by wood and coal. Regular service of a new electric railroad, called the San Francisco Vallejo and Napa Valley Railroad Company, began in 1908 and ended in 1933. A nostalgic trip on the electric train took place in 1938, with riders dressed in early 20th-century costume and historic displays of memorabilia. This photograph was taken before removal of the rails on Main Street in 1942, when steel scrap was needed for World War II. (Courtesy of Jack and Marcey Smith.)

The first St. Helena Public Library began by private subscription in 1875. The library became city owned in 1892 and was housed in the Oddfellows building. With funds donated by Andrew Carnegie, a new building was completed in 1908 in the California mission style. With great fanfare, the Native Sons and the Women's Improvement Club (now the Federated Women's Club) planted the palm trees in 1909, naming them Colonel Sutter and Colonel Vallejo. The building, located at Oak Avenue and Adams Street, served as the library until 1979. (Courtesy of Jack and Marcey Smith.)

This aerial view is of the 1951 Harvest Festival parade and displays engines from the St. Helena Fire Department. The photograph shows that buildings have new tenants. On the left are the Signal Gas Station, Purity Grocery (Steves Hardware), and Danny Kay Cleaners (Steves Housewares). On the right are B. L. Taylor Appliance (Vasconi's Pharmacy) and Mickey's Bar (St. Helena Olive Oil Company). A sign points to Carpy Field and Gray Gables Hotel on Adams Street. (Courtesy of the St. Helena Fire Department.)

Bard Suverkrop captured these scenes of downtown in 1951. The photograph above shows Main Street looking north from the Sulphur Creek bridge. In 1921, Oscar and Martin Anderson moved their business to the corner of Main and Pope Streets. They repaired cars and sold tires and gasoline until 1945 when the business morphed into an appliance store. Visible are Albert Myers's Chevrolet dealership, the Texaco service station, and J. C. Stansberry's Ford dealership. The photograph to the right shows Bank of America, Family Beverage, Kirkpatrick's 5 and 10, Smith's Pharmacy, Pacific Gas and Electric, Model Bakery, and Mickey's Bar on the west side of Main Street. (Photographs courtesy of the Napa Valley Wine Library Association.)

From 1883 to 1891, St. Helena City Hall was located on Oak Avenue and Tainter Street, and then was moved to this building on Main Street, north of Adams Street. In 1953, a bond issue was passed to construct the present-day city hall on Main and Pine Streets. In September 1954, the firemen removed the fire bell until it could be placed at the new firehouse. The old city hall gave way to a parking lot. (Courtesy of the St. Helena Fire Department.)

In September 1954, photographers for Standard Oil Company's magazine staged a photo shoot on Main Street to illustrate the benefits of petroleum to small-town America. Here is a shot of the city's official vehicles, including fire, police, ambulance, and school busses. The man on the high platform is Jon Brenner, one of the top photographers of the day. The magazine was circulated to 232,000 readers. (Courtesy of the St. Helena Fire Department.)

Three

FUN AND MOVIES

The St. Helena Brass Band, organized in 1884, had 11 members and received regular accolades in the *St. Helena Star*. In front on the ground, from left to right, are Frank Hoffman and Leigh Bierce (son of author Ambrose Bierce). Standing, from left to right, are Louis Clark, O. H. Blank, two unidentified, Jordan Jessen, Victor Gallatin, Fritz Graf, unidentified, and Adolph Bussenius. (Courtesy of Gail Palmer Morgan.)

This photograph shows a parade making its way down Main Street on July 4, 1885. Parade participants marched to Hunt's Grove, where the volunteer firemen (the parade's organizers) served Napa Valley wines, food, and ice cream. Music was provided by bands from Napa and St. Helena. (Courtesy of the Taplin and Wight families.)

On July 4, 1888, a grand parade took place on Main Street. Mariano Bale (son of Edward Turner Bale) was the parade's grand marshal. Among the participants were the U.S. Marine Band; the Native Sons and Daughters; St. Helena Hook and Ladder; Bacchus, God of Wine; St. Helena Turnverein (the German social club); the city council; and residents riding in carriages dressed up as pioneers. Shown here are members of the Americus Hose Company No. 2, who are, from left to right, (first row, kneeling) Willie Hoffman, Al Bell, and Mr. Cox; (second row, standing) Joe Galewsky, Richard Rammers, Ed Johnson, Willard Gibbs, Billie Caughey, Mr. Sharp, and Mr. Kilahan. (Courtesy of the St. Helena Fire Department.)

The 1891 Vintner's Festival was organized by the St. Helena Turnverein. Guests arrived by train and were feted with a concert at Turnverein Hall (see also pages 21 and 105). The second day of the festival included a parade to Edge Hill Park on Sulphur Springs Avenue and a musical picnic for 600 people. The wine grotto (above) earned $125 in sales. On the last day, there was a tour of the area, with stops for wine tasting, food, and singing. In 1892, a parade from Turnverein Hall—which included members of the Calistoga Brass Band, Napa County Swiss Club, Grand Army of the Republic, Turnverein, and merry picnickers (below)—again marched to Edge Hill Park, where games were played and hot air balloon rides were given. Dancing lasted until midnight, and the event was pronounced a grand success. (Above photograph courtesy of the Frank and Edith Harrison Trust; below photograph courtesy of Jack and Marcey Smith.)

A triumphal arch, shown here, was erected by the St. Helena Native Sons of the Golden West for the September 9, 1903, Admission Day parade. The two-day holiday began with a concert by the Napa Native Sons Band. The next day featured the parade, "fully four blocks long," with Calistoga, Napa, and Vallejo Native Sons participating. The party afterward included speeches, band music, a baseball game, and dancing until midnight. (Courtesy of the Napa County Historical Society.)

The July 4, 1905, parade was organized by the St. Helena Women's Improvement Club (now the Federated Women) and the board of trade (now the chamber of commerce). Sitting in the front of the carriage from left to right are Laura Walker (secretary) and Lucy Mackinder (vice president); in the back are Hannah Weinberger (president) and Mrs. Gutzwiller (treasurer). After the parade, everyone moved to Hunt's Grove for a celebration. (Courtesy of Historic Photos Publishers.)

In this photograph, the tracks down the middle of the street indicate that it was taken after electric trains began running in 1908. The marchers' military uniforms suggest that this was an event to celebrate Decoration Day, the precursor to Memorial Day. The stone building to the right houses the *St. Helena Star* and the post office. (Courtesy of the George and Elsie Wood St. Helena Public Library.)

The four-day Vintage Festival, held in 1912 and sponsored by the chamber of commerce, put St. Helena on the map. The organizers were, from left to right, (first row, seated) H. Taubner Goethe (program), Frank B. Mackinder (publicity; see pages 29, 60, 70, and 85), Mark Bruck (exhibits), and Walter Metzner (sponsors; see pages 53, 70, and 125); (second row, standing) Tom Boalt (transportation and accommodations), Gardner DeVeuve (chairman, decorations), Al Bell (music and dances), Frank Alexander (concessions), and Harry Chinn (finances). (Courtesy of Historic Photos Publishers.)

The second Vintage Festival was held over a four-day period in September 1913. Parade participants are lined up in front of the train depot for a photograph. Pictured at left are the St. Helena Grammar School's "Fairyland" boat under sail and the St. Helena Native Sons' wagon with the St. Helena Native Daughters of the Golden West dressed up as Roman goddesses.

The Spanish missionaries who planted the first wine grapes in California are represented on the wagon at left. On the wagon with the banner is Ivy Loeber representing St. Helena and surrounded by girls in costumes representing the four great wine countries: France, Italy, Spain, and Germany. On horseback are riders of the Redmen Lodge, a fraternal organization whose members studied and admired Native American ways. (Courtesy of the Molinari family.)

Queen Lily Paulson presided over the Vintage Festival held in 1914. These wine-themed events lasted several days, attracting thousands of people to town. The festival included viticultural and horticultural exhibits, the staging of *Vintage Allegory*, and "the finest industrial and floral parade ever seen in Napa County." (Courtesy of Historic Photos Publishers.)

The *Vintage Allegory* cast of 1915 poses here, with reigning queen Bertha Harris in the center. The play was written by Gardner DeVeuve (principal of the elementary school) and portrayed the history of the vine. It told of the threatened destruction of the vineyards by phylloxera and how growers were saved by Uncle Sam, who introduced a resistant vine. (Courtesy of Noelle French Peterson.)

The St. Helena Concert Band often provided music for dances and local events. This photograph shows band members in front of the St. Helena Grammar School. Pictured, from left to right, are (first row, kneeling) director D. O. Reavis, Arthur Schroeder, Frank Delaney, and Warren Steves; (second row, standing) Martin Anderson, Edwin Paulson, Frank Harrison (see also page 68), Harry Prouty, Albert Werle, Ernest Box, Louis G. Clark Jr., Louis G. Clark Sr., unidentified, Walter Lenz, Tony Caldera, Bob Prouty, unidentified, Peter Molinari, Charlie Delaney, and Willard Paulson. (Courtesy of the Frank and Edith Harrison Trust.)

Frank "Hippo" Warren, a large, jovial man, was the night policeman in town. Here, around 1920, dressed in women's attire and snugly fitting into the seat of the pony cart, he delights the crowd. (Courtesy of the St. Helena Historical Society.)

The American Legion float in the July 4, 1930, parade is covered with poppies recalling the bloodshed of World War I and the poem "In Flanders Fields": "The poppies blow, between the crosses row on row, that mark our place; and in the sky the larks, still bravely singing, fly scarce heard amid the guns below." (Courtesy of the St. Helena Historical Society.)

The United Ancient Order of Druids (UAOD) started in America in 1830. The guiding virtues of the St. Helena chapter, called a circle, were honor, truth, justice, faith, hope, love, and benevolence. This is the UAOD Olive Circle No. 8 float in the July 4, 1930, parade. (Courtesy of the St. Helena Historical Society.)

Sophia Werle Korte (see also page 91) rides a tricycle in the July 4, 1930, parade. To the right is a bicyclist sponsored by the Old Mill Service Station. The St. Helena fire truck is the 1917 Schneer still driven in parades today. (Courtesy of the St. Helena Historical Society.)

Having fun while being thrifty was the order of the day during the Depression. Here the "Spirits of St. Helena" buggy proudly states, "We use Ethyl" (for horsepower) at the Fourth of July parade around 1930. (Courtesy of the St. Helena Historical Society.)

The 1934 Vintage Festival, held for three days in September, was attended by at least 40,000 people. The parade included this entry depicting the end of Prohibition, which was described as follows in the *St. Helena Star*: "An ancient hearse drawn by two mules carried the corpse of old man depression. The drivers wore silk hats in the funeral style of the 1880s and behind dangled a bottle of wine." (Courtesy of the Frank and Edith Harrison Trust.)

The 1934 Vintage Festival parade included a float for the new queen, Evelyn Doak. The St. Helena 20-30 Club float followed, consisting of a huge bottle pouring wine, under which two lovely ladies sat in a coach. A little girl was seated on the bottle. The club won first prize for its ingenuity. (Courtesy of Ida Merla Porterfield.)

50

John McCormick, Mario Vasconi, and Joe Vasconi are shown during the 1934 Vintage Festival parade. John is riding alongside the stagecoach that had previously carried passengers over the Old Toll Road between Calistoga and towns in Lake County. Passengers are dressed in the garb of the 1880s. The Richie Block is in the background (see also page 20). (Courtesy of Ida Merla Porterfield.)

Here is the Vintage Festival barrel-roll contest on Adams Street in 1935. This is the final heat. Contestants were, from left to right, Dennis Gagetta for himself, Alex Brovelli for Greystone, Roy Raymond for Beringer, Everett Hall for To-Kalon, and Steve Jackse for Salmina. Roy Raymond won first place, followed by Jackse, Gagetta, and Brovelli. (Courtesy of Ida Merla Porterfield.)

The Vintage Festival parade in 1935 was led by Captain Critchley of the highway patrol, followed by police chief C. C. Johnson in an automobile and grand marshal Sheriff Jack Steckter on a black horse. Subsequent bands, drill teams, cowpunchers, and commercial floats drew cheers from the crowd. The Beringer Brothers Winery float was this truck laden with wine casks and decorated with silver leaves and grapes. (Courtesy of Ida Merla Porterfield.)

More than 200 singers and dancers dressed in old-world costumes were part of the 1935 Vintage Festival pageant. The dancers performed gypsy, Italian, and German dances. From left to right are Jewell Smith McKenna, Ann Lawrence, Constance Monharsh, Thora Bacher, Alice Forkum, Eunice Gibbs, Elvira Norman, and Lois Bagwill. (Courtesy of the George and Elsie Wood St. Helena Public Library.)

Gee Gee's Bar was located on Hunt Avenue opposite Railroad Avenue in the old St. Helena Brewery building. Felix "Gee Gee" Freilone and his wife, Frances, opened the establishment in 1934 after Prohibition ended. Serving beer and home-cooked food, it was a local hangout for over 30 years. Shown here are Gee Gee and Frances with customers in 1944. (Courtesy of Jack and Marcey Smith.)

Mayor Walter Metzner (see also pages 43, 70, and 125) opened the Mexican Independence Day celebration on September 16, 1947, at the Native Sons Hall by commending Mexico for sending 700 men to harvest crops during wartime. Other speakers were Lucio Perez, Zebedeo Garcia, Ralph Hayos, Paul Landeros, Enriqueta Perez, Filiberto Castillo, and Juan Torres. After songs by Pedro Nava, the Aguirre Sisters, and Rafael Rodriguez (at center in photograph and see page 72) and friends, the dancing began to a Latin American orchestra from San Francisco. (Courtesy of Rafael Rodriguez.)

The Vintage Festival held on October 16, 1949, was the first after a 14-year break. The three-hour event at Carpy Field was attended by a crowd of about 3,000 people. On the stage, from left to right, are Mary Bianchi (as Queen of the Grapes), Father O'Connor (the Catholic priest who blessed the grapes), Oreste Seragnoli (portraying Father Serra), unidentified, Roy Schoepf, Charles Constantini (of the chamber of commerce), Antoinette Spinoza (as Queen of St. Helena), and others unidentified. The afternoon was filled with music and folk dancing. (Courtesy of the George and Elsie Wood St. Helena Public Library.)

The St. Helena Municipal Band held its annual reunion at Walter Lenz's home until 1959, when Walter died. Around 1950, attendees were, from left to right, Peter Molinari (kneeling), Martin Signorelli, D. O. Reavis, Frank Harrison (see also pages 68 and 111), unidentified, Walter Lenz, and another unidentified (kneeling). (Courtesy of the Molinari family.)

On September 15, 1950, the candidates for the queen of the Harvest Days Festival posed at Mardikian's ranch (now Quintessa). They are, from left to right, Helen Defilipis, Alberta Galleron (chosen to be queen), Joyce Giugni, Charlotte Tilton, Anita Bosetti, Norma Simmons, Gwen Sciutto, and Ora Lee Fontana. Managed by the St. Helena Junior Women's Club, the contest began with a variety show, and then queen hopefuls modeled in swimsuits, casual clothes, and evening gowns before the winner was announced. (Courtesy of the George and Elsie Wood St. Helena Public Library.)

On Saturday, October 3, 1953, the Harvest Days Festival offered the usual variety show and selection of a queen, followed by a dance. This photograph captures the parade down Main Street on Sunday, as it passed Adams Street. A bond to replace the rickety city hall was on the ballot that autumn, prompting the entry at left (see also pages 21 and 38). (Courtesy of the St. Helena Fire Department.)

The Centennial Harvest Days Festival celebrated the 1854 founding of St. Helena with three days of fun in October 1954. It began on Friday with softball games between merchants on the east and west sides of Main Street, followed on Saturday by the Centennial Pageant and the Harvest Ball. On Sunday, there was a large parade with over 70 entries. Here the St. Helena Fire Department's Ed Penland and Eddie Bonhote (see pages 33 and 61) drive the 1917 Schneer fire truck. (Courtesy of the St. Helena Fire Department.)

Rafael Rodriguez (pictured at left; see also page 72) gives Rock Hudson a viticulture lesson at Inglenook Winery during the filming of *This Earth Is Mine* in 1958. More than half of the film was shot in the vineyards and wineries of Napa Valley, including Inglenook, Charles Krug, Beaulieu, Louis Martini, and Schramsberg. Jean Simmons, Claude Rains, and Dorothy McGuire also starred in the movie. (Courtesy of Rafael Rodriguez.)

On August 7, 1959, filming began in St. Helena for the Walt Disney classic *Pollyanna*, starring Haley Mills (pictured), Jane Wyman, Richard Egan, Nancy Olson, Kevin Corcoran, and Karl Malden. The sites used in the movie were the Southern Pacific Railroad depot, the Sulphur Creek railroad trestle, and Napa River at Zinfandel Lane. (Courtesy of Yolanda Pincus.)

Ken and Alice Taplin and their children, Melinda and Stephen, were extras in the movie. Little Bill came along for the fun. Mayor Louis Stralla appointed Ken to be in charge of the antique cars, including his 1913 Model T Ford. In August, summer weather made the heavy Victorian costumes uncomfortably hot. Other local extras were Fred and Petite Abruzzini, Bebe York, and Edna Johnson. (Courtesy of the Taplin and Wight families.)

Elvis Presley came to town to film *Wild in the Country* on November 11, 1960. Some of the filming took place in Sulphur Creek near the high school. The whole student body skipped school and walked over to watch. Some fans were able to see filming in the Napa River near Big Tree Road at the Battuello ranch, where Elvis posed for the photograph below. To the left, the King signs autographs for Ms. Powell (back left), Ms. Youngreen (front left), and other admirers. Altogether about 80 Hollywood people came to the valley. The principal film location was the Ink House, located on California State Route 29 at Whitehall Lane. Other stars were Hope Lange, Tuesday Weld, and John Ireland. The movie portrays the troubles of a country boy (Elvis) in the South. The crew moved back to Los Angeles to finish interiors at the Twentieth Century Fox studios. (Photographs courtesy of Yolanda Pincus.)

Four

PEOPLE

On February 16, 1950, about 350 St. Helena baseball fans gathered at Native Sons Hall to meet members of the Seals, a San Francisco ball club. Locals, from left to right, are (first row) Ted Schneider, Bob Pestoni, Eddie Salvestrin, Douglas Hystedt, Danny Thomas, and Mason Hoberg; (second row) Dr. Jim Salmon (club trainer), Joe Orenzo (club manager), Al Carpy (local baseball organizer), Joe Spring (Seals coach), Teddy Salarese (pitcher), and Al Fioresi (chief scout). (Courtesy of the Salvestrin family.)

Starr Baldwin (see also page 127) was synonymous with the *St. Helena Star* for almost 50 years. After gaining journalism experience elsewhere, he moved to town in 1934 and began working for his stepfather, Frank B. Mackinder, at the *Star* (see also pages 29, 43, 70, and 85). Baldwin photographed almost every event and sport in town. He was named St. Helena Citizen of the Year in 1972. When he was 78 (1977), he sold the newspaper to the Brenner family. (Courtesy of the St. Helena Historical Society.)

The Beringer Winery is the legacy of two brothers, Frederick and Jacob. The home, once owned by David Hudson, became that of Jacob and Agnes Beringer, shown here with their offspring before 1915. Their children managed the winery; pictured, from left to right, are Otto (cellar master), Agnes, Charles (president), Martha (bottling), Bertha (secretary/manager), and Jacob Jr. (foreman). The Hudson House remains part of the Beringer Winery today (see also page 85). (Courtesy of Historic Photos Publishers.)

Mary Geneva Eckfeldt (shown at right) became Eddie Bonhote's wife in 1912. The children were Aileen (Saviez) (left; see also page 98) and Louis. Mary was known as a fine hatmaker and for her dedication to the Red Cross. She also served as the town's librarian. Eddie Bonhote (shown below; see also pages 33 and 56) was born in Rutherford, went to school in St. Helena, and worked in the bicycle or automobile repair business all his life. He began working for Grant's Garage in 1902 and bought the business from Philo Grant in 1927. He served as assistant chief and secretary of St. Helena's volunteer fire department for 50 years. Bonhote was also active in the St. Helena Rotary Club and the Napa Valley Masonic Lodge No. 93, and he served as treasurer of the St. Helena Cemetery Association. The Bonhotes were active members of Grace Episcopal Church. (Photographs courtesy of Historic Photos Publishers.)

Bismarck "Mark" Bruck (see also pages 43, 82, and 105) was the grandson of Edward Turner Bale, an upper Napa Valley land grantee. Mark grew up at the Bale adobe on Whitehall Lane. From 1984 on, he managed Charles Krug Winery and leased it from the Krug family in 1918. Besides making wine, he ran a large grapevine nursery; was a town, school, and library trustee; and a county supervisor. This 1914 photograph was taken when he won a seat in the state assembly. (Courtesy of Kergan Bruck.)

Albert "Al" Carpy's family owned Greystone Cellars and lived in the adjoining manor house. For many years, the Carpys lent their pool for Red Cross swim lessons. Al organized the Carpy Gang (which is still going strong) in 1936, which consisted of a group of young boys and some girls who played baseball, basketball, and football, and also held boxing matches. Al and his daughter, Mathilde, are shown here. (Courtesy of Historic Photos Publishers.)

Fortune Chevalier (left), with Eveline and son, George Chevalier, is shown here before 1899. The F. Chevalier Company, established in 1857, became a large San Francisco wholesale liquor dealer. After George turned his business over to George Jr. in 1883, Fortune came to St. Helena in 1887 and built a home on his 191-acre ranch. Fortune built the Chateau Chevalier Winery and planted vineyards on Spring Mountain (see also page 18). (Courtesy of Kay Bissonette.)

George Belden Crane (1806–1898) was a native of New York. After receiving his medical degree, he moved to California in 1853. His study of European viticulture and soil types led him to conclude that St. Helena was the perfect location to plant grapes. George bought 300 acres and planted "foreign" vines where St. Helena High School is now, building a winery in 1860. (Courtesy of the St. Helena Historical Society.)

Paulin and Lucie DeLord (see also page 80) operated a shoe shop for more than 50 years (1900–1953). Paulin learned his trade in his native France, coming to San Francisco in 1893 at the age of 18. The DeLords bought the Elgin home located at 1326 Oak Avenue (see page 80). (Courtesy of Historic Photos Publishers.)

This group is picnicking at James Dowdell's hopfield in 1892. An Irish immigrant who came to California via Panama in 1869, Dowdell settled in St. Helena and planted hops in 1873. A fire burned his barn, hop house, and 188 bales of hops in 1884. In 1887, when Chinese hop pickers went on strike, growers switched to white teenage laborers. These girls are probably visiting, as they are not dressed for fieldwork. From left to right are (first row, on ground) May Wells, Alice Fifield, Mamie Warren, and Lucy Warren; (second row, on ground) unidentified, Josie Anderson, Tillie Heyman, Viola Rhinfrank, Louise Rhinfrank, Charley Jessen, Gertie Grigsby, and Katherine Dowdell (see also page 91); (third row, standing) all unidentified. (Courtesy of Gail Palmer Morgan.)

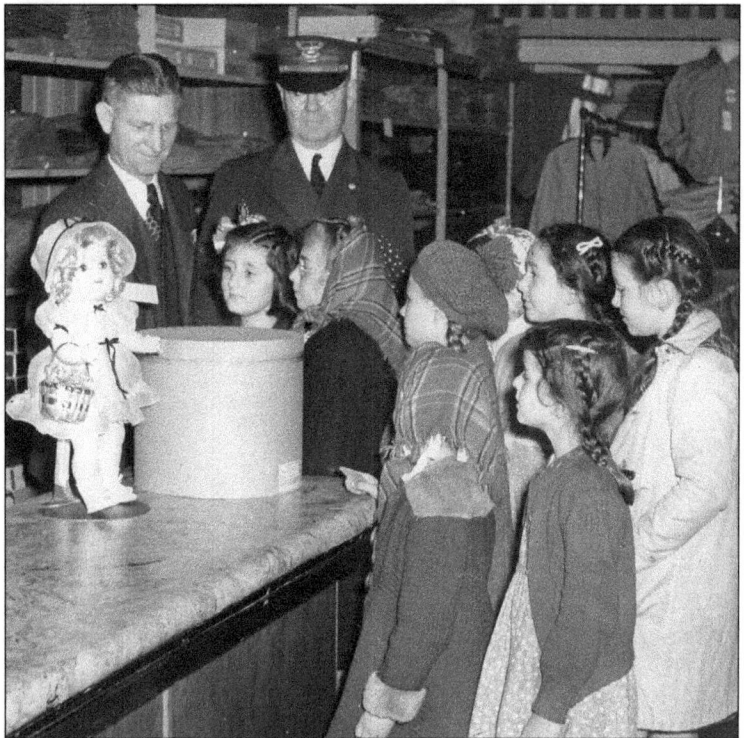

This drawing for a doll prize to raise money for the Red Cross in 1942 is overseen by Judge Louis D. Vasconi (left; see also page 108) and police chief Chaney Johnson (see also page 82). Judge Vasconi founded an insurance agency and was appointed to the local court. Johnson served the town for 46 years as constable, tax collector, and fire marshal. The girls at far right are Jenny Paris, Helen Paris, and Joanne Kirkpatrick. The doll and her wardrobe were prepared by Jean Spear. (Courtesy of the Clyde Kirkpatrick Collection.)

These children are, from left to right, Oliver, Dorothea, and Melvin Eisan, whose parents were Frank and Lena Eisan (see also page 87). Frank was a prominent walnut rancher in the area. Oliver became a pharmacist but was killed as a prisoner of war during World War II. Dorothea was once named queen of the Napa County Fair. Melvin managed the family ranch and bought Ted's Toggery in 1956, changing the name to Mel's Clothing. (Courtesy of Historic Photos Publishers.)

In 1853, William and Mary Elgin arrived in California by wagon train. In 1857, William opened a general store, adding a livery business in 1866. William served the community in many capacities for 54 years. The couple had five children: Ira, Clarence, Alice, Sarah, and Jessie. William and Mary are shown here on their 60th wedding anniversary in 1911. (Courtesy of Historic Photos Publishers.)

This circle of friends is gathered on the porch of the Gray Gables Hotel (see also pages 34 and 101). Pictured, from left to right, are (first row) Mary Andresen Elgin, a Mrs. Cruey, three unidentified women, and Mrs. Davis; (second row) Maggie Outwaters (the hostess), Sophie "Tante" Wageman, a second Mrs. Cruey, Sophie Alstrom Mitchell, Mrs. Irvin Wilson, unidentified, and Carrie Adsit. (Courtesy of the George and Elsie Wood St. Helena Public Library.)

Rinaldo "Ray" Ghiringhelli is shown behind the bar at Ray's Place, where Ana's Cantina is now located. He was born in San Francisco and educated in St. Helena, and for a time he worked at Mickey's Bar with Roy Schoepf. For 22 years (until he retired due to illness), Ghiringhelli was the "host of Main Street," and Ray's Place was a second home to many. Ghiringhelli died in 1970. (Courtesy of the Ghiringhelli-Rehe family.)

Wesley "Jinks" Jennings (1892–1980) lived in St. Helena all of his life, except for the time he served in World War I. Jennings had great mechanical and electrical skills. He probably built the first radio in St. Helena, on which friends listened avidly to ball games. Working for a private contractor and then the city, he helped maintain the electrolier streetlights along Main Street. (Courtesy of Historic Photos Publishers.)

Boyhood friends Perry Blake, Frank Harrison (see also pages 54 and 111), Leo Harrison, and Lionel Blake are shown, from left to right, traveling to the coast in 1920. Perry sold real estate and insurance and became city treasurer. Frank owned a candy manufacturing business in San Francisco. Leo learned the printing trade at the *St. Helena Star*, later working in San Francisco. Lionel became a banker. (Courtesy of the Frank and Edith Harrison Trust.)

Pictured here is the Lazzari family in 1885, from left to right, as follows: the children, Lena and Josephine, with parents, Angelina and Frank. After becoming widowed, Angelina married Angelo Signorello, who helped her operate the Roma Hotel, which is Cindy's Backtreet Kitchen today. Angelina was a master of Italian cuisine and catered most of the banquets in town. Lena married building contractor Wilbur Harrison. (Courtesy of the Frank and Edith Harrison Trust.)

Harvey Lewelling (see also page 22), shown in 1885, was an amateur photographer who took many photographs of the St. Helena area in the 1880s. He used a large, bulky camera and heavy glass plates, which had to be developed quickly before the emulsions collapsed. He was president of the Bank of St. Helena for 25 years and also managed the family vineyards. (Courtesy of the Taplin and Wight families.)

Harvey Lewelling and John C. Money (see also page 86) built the first gasoline-powered car in St. Helena in 1894. The driver sat at the rear, where he steered through the use of levers. The car traveled only a few hundred yards and made such a fearsome noise that it was banned from the roads. Shown here is a Lewelling ranch worker (unidentified, left) with Ethel Lewelling and dog, Shep. Ethel married Albert Taplin. (Courtesy of the Taplin and Wight families.)

Frank B. Mackinder bought the *St. Helena Star* newspaper in 1885 and owned it for over 50 years, becoming known for his editorials. He was active in the Presbyterian church and was a charter member and second president of the St. Helena Rotary Club. He was also postmaster, a member of St. Helena Masonic Lodge No. 93, a member of Rutherford Grange No. 371, and president of the St. Helena Cemetery Association. He died in 1937. (See also pages 29, 43, and 85.) (Courtesy of the St. Helena Historical Society.)

Walter Metzner (see also pages 43, 53, and 125) became a pharmacist, and in 1903, he married Susan Smith, daughter of the Smith's Pharmacy founder. Walter owned the pharmacy from 1912 to 1949 and then joined his brother in the real estate business. Walter was mayor of St. Helena for 16 years and served four more years on the city council. He was called Mr. Rotary because of his long service to that club. He died in 1965. (See also page 127.) (Courtesy of Historic Photos Publishers.)

John C. Money (see also page 86) poses here with his granddaughter, Dean. John was a well-known building contractor who built many bridges and homes in town. He served the town council for over 40 years as street superintendent, building inspector, and councilman. John and Sarah Money's daughter, Helen, married Ellery Murray. The Murrays' daughter, Dean, married Campbell Wilson. John Money died in 1944; Money Lane is named after him. (Courtesy of Historic Photos Publishers.)

William York was one of the area's earliest settlers, participating in the Bear Flag Revolt of 1846. He is pictured with his daughter, Clara Palmer, and wife, Frances Mills York. In his arms is his grandson, Lowell Palmer. Pictured in the front are other grandchildren, Esther Palmer (Thompson) and Ray Palmer. Esther's grandson is U.S. congressman Mike Thompson. (Courtesy of Gail Morgan Lane.)

Gunilda "Jean" Pistorius was born to German parents in 1907. Shown here in a high school graduation photograph in 1925, she attended nursing school and was a public health nurse for 25 years in San Francisco. In 1952, she married Walter Rianda and returned to St. Helena, where she was a realtor for over 30 years. Two homes that she owned became the Rianda House Senior Activity Center and the Red Cross headquarters. (Courtesy of Historic Photos Publishers.)

Rafael Rodriguez (right) and a friend took a ride to Angwin and posed for a picture at the vista point in 1944. When Rafael came to Napa Valley, he first worked at the Emmolo Packing Company, later at the Emmolo Grapevine Nursery. He went on to manage vineyards for several large wineries. Rafael was always interested in community affairs; he served as a St. Helena school trustee and in Hispanic community service organizations. (See also pages 53 and 57.) (Courtesy of Rafael Rodriguez.)

The annual Fireman's Ball to benefit the St. Helena Fire Department has been held for over 50 years. Traditionally, firemen sold tickets around town. Here Roberto Rojas (left) discusses a sales transaction with Charles Oliver (center), while Jess Torres (right) observes on Mountain View Avenue south of St. Helena. (Courtesy of the St. Helena Fire Department.)

John Henry Steves moved to St. Helena from Wisconsin in 1877. He had learned the tinsmith trade and bought a plumbing and hardware business when he was 27 years old. He organized the town's water company and laid many of the city's utility pipes. He ran Steves Hardware for 65 years and died in 1954 at the age of 103. (See also page 34.) (Courtesy of Historic Photos Publishers.)

73

Norman Strouse was born in 1905. For most of his career in advertising, he worked for the J. Walter Thompson Company in San Francisco. In 1969, he and his wife, Charlotte, used a large collection of Robert Louis Stevenson memorabilia to found the Robert Louis Stevenson Silverado Museum, located next to the George and Elsie Wood St. Helena Public Library. Norman was named St. Helena Citizen of the Year in 1977. (Courtesy of the Robert Louis Stevenson Silverado Museum.)

The eight-year-old boy called Indian Tobe was removed from his tribe on the Eel River by vengeful whites who killed many of the tribe. He was adopted by the Money family and grew up on the Money ranch near Oakville. He made his living as a barber in St. Helena and lived in a house near Sulphur Creek. He died in 1931. (Courtesy of the John C. Money family.)

In 1849, Israel Warren sailed from Massachusetts to San Francisco on his way to look for gold. In 1852, he and his family settled in St. Helena, where he became a carpenter and cabinetmaker. Israel is shown (first row, left) before his death in 1905. His grandchild, Lois, is standing in front of his daughter, Anne, and his son, Oliver, is standing to the right. (Courtesy of the St. Helena Historical Society.)

Hannah Rabbe married John Weinberger in 1871. They built their home and winery north of St. Helena, next to today's St. Clement Winery. John was very involved in the community and a director of the Bank of St. Helena. After he was murdered in 1882, Hannah managed the winery and won awards for her wine. She took his seat on the Bank of St. Helena board of directors and was elected founding president of the Women's Improvement Club in 1905. A devoted Presbyterian, Hannah died in 1931 at age 90. (See also page 86.) (Courtesy of Historic Photos Publishers.)

Dr. George Wood was born in North Dakota in 1896 and moved to California in 1908. In 1913, he began his studies at the University of California, Berkeley. In 1926, he joined his brother, Frank, who was farming in St. Helena. Doctor Wood delivered more than 2,000 babies, many of whom attended Doctor Wood Appreciation Day in 1987. Named St. Helena Citizen of the Year in 1973, his medical colleagues honored him as a "model of a rural county practitioner." At the age of 90, he retired after 61 years of serving St. Helena. (Courtesy of the George and Elsie Wood St. Helena Public Library.)

George met Elsie when she was a nurse at St. Gothard's Hospital (now the Grandview Apartments; see also page 32). The Woods were supporters of education and provided scholarships for local college students. After his wife's death in 1972, George started the Elsie Wood Memorial Scholarship. When the library began a building fund, he led the campaign to build the new library, which is named in his and his wife's honor. George endowed the George and Elsie Wood Trust, which provides extra services and materials to the library. He died in 1997 at the age of 101. (Courtesy of the George and Elsie Wood St. Helena Public Library.)

Five

HISTORIC HOMES

The Madrona Heights building lots on Spring Mountain Road were offered by agents W. A. Mackinder and C. H. Anderson. In 1900, William Bell moved into the corner house (left) at Madrona Avenue. William and Alphonse Bell owned Bell Brothers clothing store in town for 40 years. The house was built by Gustav Jursch, who constructed many fine homes. Jursch built the third house (far right) in 1905 for Frank and Lucy Mackinder (see also page 70). (Courtesy of Historic Photos Publishers.)

An unusual snowstorm blanketed the town on January 15, 1932. In 1877, banker-merchant D. B. Carver and his family moved into their new home (left). The Carver mansion was demolished in 1940 to make way for the post office. Joseph Tosetti worked at Rossi and Anderson's general store for 35 years. His family lived at 1475 Main Street (right) for over 20 years, which is now the Rianda House Senior Activity Center. (Courtesy of the Frank and Edith Harrison Trust.)

The home of pioneer Col. Joseph Chiles, on Spring Street next to the Native Sons Hall, was built in 1874, so his children could attend school in town. Sitting in the buggy are Henry L. Chiles and Mary Tully Kenyon. In the background are (left) Leonard Tully; (right) Elizabeth Chiles and Margaret Chiles. In 1949, the Baptist church converted the home to its sanctuary. (Courtesy of Gail Morgan Lane.)

78

In 1859, Dr. George Belden Crane purchased property in St. Helena. He was the first to plant European grape varieties and became a Napa Valley wine pioneer. At the time, Sunny Acres was a simple farmhouse, but in 1879 it was enlarged to the Victorian home it is today. In 1932, John Salvestrin, a northern Italian immigrant, bought the 26-acre Crane parcel, and Salvestrins still occupy Sunny Acres today. Some of the original Crane furnishings remain at Sunny Acres. The parlor museum displays numerous photographs of Dr. Crane and his wife, Frances; their piano, which came around Cape Horn in 1849; and several pieces of their furniture. During the restoration of Sunny Acres, a time capsule was found that contained a letter written by Frances Crane, along with numerous social cards and newspapers of the day. (Photographs courtesy of the Salvestrin family.)

This was the home of William A. Elgin, who arrived in town in 1857 and opened one of the first general stores. He was a county supervisor from 1859 to 1861. He was also a justice of the peace, town trustee, and postmaster. In 1920, French immigrants Paulin and Lucie DeLord bought the property. They owned a shoe store on Main Street until 1953 (see page 64), and their descendants own the home today. (Courtesy of Gail Morgan Lane.)

This home was originally owned by Antonio and Mariana Forni. Antonio came to this country from Italy in 1876. In 1886, he married Mariana in Italy and returned with her to St. Helena to open Europa House Saloon with Luigi Vasconi (see also page 20). Later he operated a winery called Lombarda Cellars (now Freemark Abbey north of St. Helena). For many years, the Fornis' daughter, Inez, and husband, Bart Supple, lived in the home. (Courtesy of the Napa County Historical Society.)

This home, located at the corner of Elmhurst Avenue and Main Street, was built by William Parmer Fuller, of paint company fame. In 1880, his household included his wife, six children, a gardener, two Chinese servants, and a nurse. Three of the Fuller sons followed their father into the paint business. Later residents were the Tomkin, Jensen, Wright, and Deane families. The home is still one of the finest on Main Street. (Courtesy of Historic Photos Publishers.)

A native of Vermont, David Fulton arrived in St. Helena in 1852. He bought 40 acres in 1860 and married Mary Lyon in 1863. The following year, he built this home, which is still standing today on Fulton Lane. The property remains in the family, next to the old David Fulton Winery. In the photograph, from left to right, are Mary Fulton, Doris Rann, unidentified, Lizzie Rann Ernul, and Ida Fulton Mather. (Courtesy of the St. Helena Historical Society.)

The Johnson residence is shown here in 1909, located on Main Street north of Madrona Avenue. James George "J. G." Johnson and his wife, Alice, arrived in St. Helena in 1884. J. G. served as town treasurer, town marshal, justice of the peace, and president of the chamber of commerce (see also page 29). The house was owned by police chief Chaney Johnson (no relation to J. G.) and his wife, Emma, from about 1942 to 1967 (see also page 65). (Courtesy of the Napa County Historical Society.)

In exchange for doing the ironwork on the Bale Mill, Florentine Kellogg was given 600 acres next to the mill and built this house in 1849. Built of hand-hewn timber, it has 15 rooms. In 1871, Rev. Theodore Lyman bought the property. His son, W. W. Lyman, lived in the house, working 125 acres of vineyard and a wine cellar. The family still owns the home. (See also pages 105 and 111.) (Courtesy of Jack and Marcey Smith.)

Horticulturalist John Lewelling owned over 300 acres south of St. Helena. He built this home on Sulphur Springs Avenue in 1870. John's love of fruit growing was the distinguishing feature of his life, but he was also an officer of several banks and corporations, and he was considered an excellent financier. The house is still owned by the family. (Courtesy of Gail Morgan Lane.)

"J. I. Logan is laying out a street 60 feet wide. He has already built three cottages," reported the *St. Helena Star* in 1875 about Charter Oak Avenue. That year Logan built his home at the corner of Main Street and Charter Oak Avenue. From 1900 to 1940, it was the home of August and Cassie Ives. In 1942, Everett and Margaret Bellani bought it and owned the home until the 1990s. (Courtesy of Gail Morgan Lane.)

John McPike took charge of a wagon train from the East to California in 1850. He then became a butcher and stock raiser, provisioning the army and the mines. In 1856, he married Mary Crane. In 1861, he bought land on Chaix Lane, where the couple built this home and raised their six children. It became the Charles Forni home in the 1940s. (Courtesy of the St. Helena Historical Society.)

George Schoenwald built this home in 1883. A German immigrant who settled in town in the 1870s, Schoenwald managed the Calistoga Hot Springs and the now defunct Del Monte Hotel in Monterey. The front porch and garden were patterned after the Del Monte. Subsequent owners were the Bliss, Allen, Spotts, Holmes, and Price-Skillings families. Susan Russell Spotts named the estate Spottswoode in honor of her late husband, Albert Spotts. He saved precious city records during the 1906 San Francisco earthquake and fire, later managing the U.S. mint. (Courtesy of the Napa County Historical Society.)

John Thomann came to California from Switzerland, eventually settling near St. Helena in 1874, where he established his winery. New prosperity allowed him to build the house shown above in 1885, with six bedrooms and a full cellar used for storing wine and other provisions. His architect, Albert Schroepfer, also designed the Beringer Rhine House (see also page 60) and Parrott's Miravalle. The property was sold in 1906 to the Leuenberger family, who renamed it Sutter Home Winery (see also page 18). The photograph below, taken between 1906 and 1926, shows flags and a piano outside, perhaps for a July 4th party. Mark Bruck (see also pages 43, 62 and 105) is at far left, Frank B. Mackinder (see also pages 70 and 122) is at far right, and the others are unidentified. (Above courtesy of the Napa County Historical Society; below courtesy of the Clyde Kirkpatrick Collection.)

"The handsome residence being erected by Mrs. M. H. Vance and Mr. and Mrs. C. H. Anderson on the hill next to York Creek and Beringer will be ready within a few weeks. Carpenters and painters will finish what is one of the finest homes in Napa Valley." The architect for the Colonial-style home was William Corlett. The contractors were John C. Money (see pages 69 and 71) and C. F. Rice. Built in 1907, the home was turned into a hotel after only four years (see page 32). (Courtesy of the Napa County Historical Society.)

Beautiful gardens graced the home of John and Hannah Weinberger. Located on California State Route 29 on a hill north of Deer Park Road, the home featured fine views of the valley. John came to California in 1869, bought 240 acres, and planted 35 of them with vines. In 1871, he married Hannah Rabbe and brought her to this new home. John was murdered in 1882, but Hannah stayed in the house until her death in 1931. The house did not survive. (See also page 75.) (Courtesy of Gail Morgan Lane.)

Six

RELIGIOUS LIFE

Sharon Baptist church was the first church in St. Helena, built in 1857 and for which Church Street is named. The first trustees were John Cyrus, Henry Owsley, and David Fulton. The building was moved to the rear of the lot (at Hunt Avenue and Church Street) in 1872. In 1929, the congregation disbanded and sold the property, which was converted to apartments and is now an office building. (Courtesy of Historic Photos Publishers.)

The first church in Napa County was built on Reason Tucker's farm (now Bothe–Napa Valley State Park) and was dedicated in 1853. It was known as the White Church (shown above) because it was the only painted building in upper Napa Valley. Methodist services began to be held at the Presbyterian church in St. Helena in 1862. The new Methodist church and parsonage (shown below) were built on Adams Street and Oak Avenue in 1867, under the tenure of Rev. W. S. Bryant. In 1873, William Angwin was appointed minister, and by 1881, the construction debt was paid off. The steel ceiling and Gothic windows were installed in 1897. Charlotte Jones, one of the first female preachers in California, served from 1930 to 1941. The parsonage was sold and moved to Spring Street in 1976. (Photographs courtesy of United Methodist Church of St. Helena.)

Fr. Peter Deyaert, originally from Belgium, was pastor of the Catholic church in Napa. Prior to 1866, he would travel to St. Helena to hold services in a private home. He supervised the home remodel that became the first St. Helena Catholic Church. Father Deyaert was known as the "walking priest" for his preferred method of travel. He officiated at the wedding of Carolina Bale and Charles Krug at Napa City on December 26, 1860. (Courtesy of St. Helena Catholic Church.)

In 1866, the first Catholic church was located in a remodeled home. By 1878, it was replaced with a new wooden chapel, which then burned to the ground in 1888. Construction of the classic English medieval-style stone church on Oak Avenue and Tainter Street (shown before 1945) began in 1889, with Fr. Renatus Becker acting as architect and contractor. Archbishop Riordan dedicated the church in 1890. Father Becker died suddenly in 1892. (Courtesy of St. Helena Catholic Church.)

Fr. Patrick Blake became pastor of the Catholic church in 1892. Here he poses (third row, center) with first communicants in 1895. Early in his pastorate, he served all of upper Napa Valley. He worked closely with the Ursuline Sisters in establishing Elmhurst Academy (see pages 99–101), and in 1905, he helped establish Holy Cross Cemetery on Spring Street. Father Blake served the parish for 29 years and died in 1921. (Courtesy of St. Helena Catholic Church.)

These are the children of Celide and Anatolio Micheli. Their father came to St. Helena in 1917 and worked at Beringer Winery. In the photograph, Velia, Aldo "Mike," and Madeline make their first communion in St. Helena Catholic Church. Velia married Nathan Brovelli, Mike married Eda Milani, and Madeline married Henry Arata. Henry and Mike operated the Pastime Club on Main Street for many years. (Courtesy of Historic Photos Publishers.)

In 1926, Sophia Werle (see also page 49) married Clemens "Clem" Korte at St. Helena Catholic Church. Their attendants, from left to right, were (second row) Theresa Korte, Joseph Korte, and Catherine Korte Rolfes. The couple entered the church to the wedding march from *Lohengrin* played by Katherine Dowdell (see also page 64). A wedding breakfast followed at Tucker Farm Center. The couple made their new home at the Korte ranch, where Clem helped his father manage the vineyard. (See also pages 11, 12, 14, 16, and 126.) (Courtesy of the St. Helena Historical Society.)

St. Helena's Catholic Young Ladies Institute was formed in 1919 as a mutual aid society. Over a thousand visitors watched the Young Ladies Institute, and some young men's groups, parade on May 21, 1933, as drill teams and drum corps from the North Bay area competed for trophies. A large Catholic Mass, luncheon, and grand ball were included in the festivities. (Courtesy of the Frank and Edith Harrison Trust.)

A devastating fire heavily damaged the St. Helena Catholic Church in 1945, miraculously leaving the stained-glass windows and stone walls intact. Firefighters and citizens rushed to remove anything portable. Guided by Fr. Timothy O'Connor, the church was restored and the walls strengthened. In 2009, a restoration and earthquake retrofit were completed, and a celebratory mass was held on August 1. (Courtesy of St. Helena Catholic Church.)

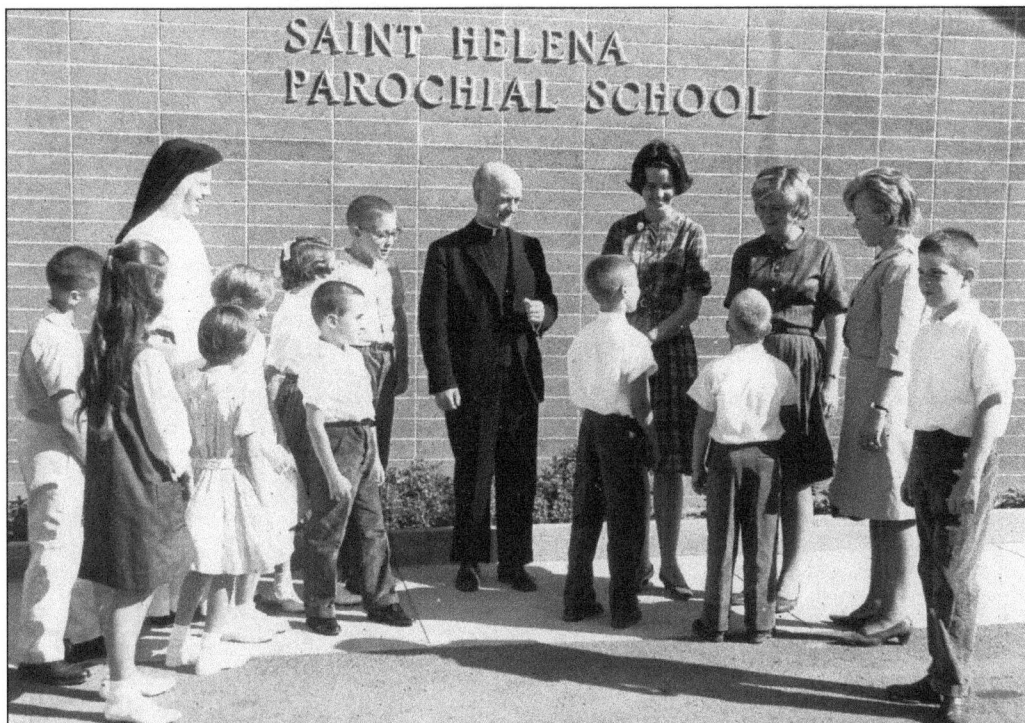

Construction of a new parochial school began in 1959 under the leadership of the newly arrived Fr. James Walsh. Although the school was finished in 1960, the opening was delayed until 1963 because of staffing issues. Under the management of the Dominican Sisters of San Rafael, the school opened in fall 1963. Here Sr. Mary Dunstan (left) and Father Walsh (center) greet students and other adults. (Courtesy of St. Helena Catholic Church.)

St. Helena has a large Spanish-speaking population, many of whom are members of the St. Helena Catholic Church's parish. A Mass in Spanish is celebrated on Sunday mornings before the mass given in English. In this photograph, the Rodriguez family chats outside the church in the 1960s. (Courtesy of Rafael Rodriguez.)

Rev. James Mitchell poses with his wife, Sophie, and sons, James (left) and John. The reverend was born in Ireland in 1841, completing his studies for the ministry in 1868. At the urging of a friend, he immigrated to California and became the Presbyterian pastor of Calistoga. In 1874, he founded the First Presbyterian Church of St. Helena. Sophie Alstrom came to San Francisco from Sweden with her mother, Marie Bremburg, in 1860. The day they arrived, her mother married Sven Alstrom, an old family friend. Sophie's new stepfather moved the family to White Sulphur Springs, which he owned, in 1862. Alstrom sold the resort and constructed the Windsor Hotel in 1881 (see also pages 19, 24, and 31). In 1883, James and Sophie were married at the Windsor. Their first son, John, was born in 1884, followed by James in 1889. John became a civil engineer and served as the city engineer of St. Helena. James became a distinguished architect in Burlingame, near San Francisco. (Courtesy of First Presbyterian Church of St. Helena.)

Sophie Mitchell (shown here in the 1930s) studied botany and painting at the Napa Ladies Seminary and became a skilled wildflower painter. She began painting as a young woman, leaving over 100 works dating from 1877 to 1939. Sophie taught at the seminary but kept her hobby quiet, since it was not acceptable for a minister's wife to sell paintings. Her husband collected wildflowers and brought them home for her to paint. She taught Sunday school, tended her garden, and for 25 years was treasurer of the Benicia Presbytery (a regional office). (Courtesy of First Presbyterian Church of St. Helena.)

Under the leadership of Reverend Mitchell, the new Presbyterian church building, located on Spring Street near Kearney Street, was dedicated on January 30, 1876. By 1881, the congregation numbered 118 members. Mitchell served as pastor for 43 years and as pastor emeritus until his death in 1926. At various times he presided over mission stations at Conn Valley, Rutherford, Yountville, and Petrified Forest. (Courtesy of First Presbyterian Church of St. Helena.)

The congregation of the First Presbyterian Church of St. Helena poses in front of its building. In 1884, the lecture hall, now called Westminster Hall, was constructed. It cost $1,500 to build and included a kitchen. The church celebrated its Silver Jubilee in May 1899. At the 35th anniversary in 1909, a special service was held, with the Rev. John Hemphill preaching. He was the college friend of Reverend Mitchell who encouraged Mitchell to come to America. In 1946, an electric Hammond organ was given in memory of the servicemen from St. Helena who served in World War II. Renovation of the sanctuary took place in the 80th year of the church (1954). Groundbreaking for a classroom, kitchen, and fireside addition took place in 1958. Below is the church in the 1960s. (Photographs courtesy of First Presbyterian Church of St. Helena.)

In early 1944, Rev. Charles Hulac (left) began to hold Presbyterian services in the Pope Valley Farm Center hall, and on May 7, the Pope Valley Presbyterian Church was established. The first elders were Lawrence Groteguth, Phillip Gridley, and George Von Garden. The first to be baptized were Rox Wilcox, Barbara Wiles, and Nancy Wiles. (Courtesy of Joe Callizo.)

Episcopal services were held in St. Helena as early as 1870, but the Episcopal church had no worship building of its own. Grace Episcopal Church obtained the lot at Spring Street and Oak Avenue in 1878. A small wooden chapel served the congregation until the stone building was completed in 1884. Bishop Wingfield did not consecrate the church until 1895—after the debt was paid off. Sarah Chase Bourn donated funds to build the stone wall enclosing the church property. (Courtesy of Historic Photos Publishers.)

To the left is the interior of Grace Episcopal Church soon after it was completed. Rev. Irving Baxter became rector of Grace Episcopal Church in 1920 and retired in 1935. Below, Reverend Baxter and Sunday schoolchildren pose on May 8, 1932, as they plant a redwood tree on the 200th birthday of George Washington. From left to right are (first row) Dorothea Eisan, two unidentified girls, Van Ballentine, Helen Ballentine, Marshall Sears, and little Jacquiline Sears; (second row) Virginia Ward, Marie Sander, Reverend Baxter, Oliver Eisan, Melvin Eisan, Roy Chavez, Louis Sander, Leland Sears, and Aileen Bonhote (Saviez) (see also page 61). (Above photograph courtesy of Marie Mason Oliver; below photograph courtesy of Grace Episcopal Church.)

Seven

SCHOOLS

In 1898, the Ursuline Sisters of Santa Rosa purchased the mansion owned by Mrs. E. F. Pope as a school for girls, Elmhurst (also called Ursuline) Academy. The property had 10 acres of lawns and gardens, with another 12 being used for dairy cows and chickens. Enrollment dropped, so in 1952, after the last class graduated, the land was divided for sale. The Robert Louis Stevenson Middle School now occupies the site of the mansion. The Seventh Day Adventists built a new church on the Main Street section in 1962. (Courtesy of the St. Helena Historical Society.)

Archbishop Riordan of San Francisco, Reverend Blake of St. Helena, and Reverend Connolly of San Francisco dedicated the chapel of the Elmhurst Academy in 1899. Reverend Blake donated statues of Our Lady, St. Joseph, and Jesus. Doctor Cleary gave a statue of St. Francis and a piano in memory of his wife. Pictured above is the Ursuline Chapel in the school. In the photograph below, students enjoy a game of tennis on the former Pope family's tennis court. (Above photograph courtesy of Mary Jane Rossi; below photograph courtesy of the Korte Family Collection.)

In 1944, classes at Elmhurst Academy pose in front of the school. From left to right are (first row, seated) Julie Ghiringhelli, Anita Ghiringhelli, Eddie Salvestrin, two unidentified, Jerry Engli, unidentified, and Patsy Martinelli; (second row) Marcella Werle, Eddie Tedeschi, three unidentified, Mary Laura Bulotti, Joseph Sagadin, two unidentified, and Carol Anne Austin; (third row) two unidentified, Bob Gagetta, Billy Thompson, Betty Rutherford, unidentified, and Mary Rose Aspesi. (Courtesy of the Ghiringhelli-Rehe family.)

The St. Helena Academy was St. Helena's high school from 1882 to 1897. It was located on Adams Street at Kearney Street. Classes were offered in bookkeeping, commercial law, Latin, and elocution. The principal was Lowell Rogers, so the school was sometimes called the Rogers Academy. The building was later converted to the Gray Gables Hotel (see also pages 34, 36, and 66), which was demolished to make way for an office complex. (Courtesy of Gail Morgan Lane.)

Teacher Mary Nicholls (second row, center) poses with her students at the Conn Valley School in the 1880s. The land for the school was donated by Connelly Conn. Emma Conn and Ivy Hobson attended all nine grades there. In 1884, the school's roof caught fire. The boys climbed on the roof while the girls filled lunch pails with water and passed them up. By the time help arrived, the fire was under control. (Courtesy of Diane Dillon.)

Lodi School on Lodi Lane was founded in 1870 after W. T. Sayward and Sam Brannan donated land for the building. The total budget for one year was $170, which included teachers' salaries. Teachers included Ida Fulton, Olga Ehlers, Hannah Weinberger, Cassie Lane, and Grova Loeber. Here students pose at the school in the 1930s, including members of the Korte family. The building later became the Lodi Farm Center. (Courtesy of the Korte Family Collection.)

The Grammar School, St. Helena, Cal.

St. Helena's grammar school was moved from Main Street and Pratt Avenue to Adams Street and Oak Avenue in 1860. Finding the small, wooden building too small, a new stone school was built in 1901, becoming the pride of the town. In 1931, it was declared unsafe during earthquakes; however, demolition proved difficult due to its solid construction. The new school, completed in 1932, is still in use today. The Carnegie-funded library building (left background) indicates that the photograph was taken after 1908. (Courtesy of Jack and Marcey Smith.)

This undated photograph shows a classroom interior of the St. Helena Grammar School. Students' work—by Helen Money (Murray), Ethel Lewelling (Taplin), Jessie Ruiz, and Raymond Ewer—can be seen on the blackboards. (Courtesy of First Presbyterian Church of St. Helena.)

The 1928 eighth-grade class poses on the steps of the St. Helena Grammar School. Principal Thomas B. Street and teacher Jasmine Raymond are standing in the center of the second row. In 1920, St. Helena, Lodi, Vineland, and Spring Valley schools were united into one. There were 300 students and 11 teachers in 1926. Mr. Street became the principal in 1922. (Courtesy of the St. Helena Historical Society.)

In the 1930s, boys pose during a *Robin Hood* production at the St. Helena Grammar School. Note Friar Tuck and Robin Hood in the center of the merry men. (Courtesy of the Peter Molinari family.)

Turnverein Hall (see also pages 21 and 40) was built in 1883 by the St. Helena Turnverein, a German social club, and was the site of many large gatherings. It was a movie theater until 1913, when a new theater was built. From 1897 to 1912, the first public high school met there. In 1923, the Lyman family (see also page 82) donated the land to the town for a park. Park commissioner Mark Bruck (see also pages 43, 62, and 82) and the Women's Improvement Club (now the Federated Women's Club) led the fund-raising to landscape the park. (Courtesy of Jack and Marcey Smith.)

These ladies pose in front of Turnverein Hall when it was St. Helena High School and the G and G Theater (see also pages 21 and 40). From left to right are Louise Overacker, Julia Anderson (Dufour), Esther Pearson, Helen Moodey (Clark), Lois Alexander (Gifford), and Gretta Grant (Cairns). (Courtesy of the George and Elsie Wood St. Helena Public Library.)

Work began on a new high school in 1912 with money from 1911 school bonds and on land donated by Frances Grayson Crane. The contractor was E. T. Thurston, and cement work was done by Harry Thorsen (center). The school, built of reinforced concrete faced with stone and roofed with slate, is in use today. The top floor housed a gymnasium and assembly hall. (Courtesy of the Harold Thorsen family.)

The annual circus was presented by the students of the high school, and the main event was the vaudeville show in the auditorium. An orchestra played, students sang, and a magician performed. The costumes were made by the sewing class. Here the clowns pose for the 1918 yearbook; the only identified boys are Lewis Walter Paulson (first row, far right) and Ellery Maxwell Murray (second row, center). (Courtesy of Historic Photos Publishers.)

Pictured here is the domestic science class for girls at the high school in 1918. Girls were taught to prepare and serve economical meals with high nutritional value. World War I austerity made it necessary to learn canning, make bread, and prepare bandages for the Red Cross. Girls also learned how to design and sew their own clothes. (Courtesy of Historic Photos Publishers.)

The high school senior play, *Mrs. Temple's Telegram*, was presented on May 21, 1918. The plot centered on a husband's excuse for being gone all night. The actors shown here, from left to right, are (first row) Thelma Croft, Carmelita Murray, Lucille Metzner, Ruth Swift, and Stella Lovering; (second row) Vincent Lawford, Ralph Paulson, Arthur Rossi, Elmer Coolidge, and Merle Turner. The high school orchestra furnished the music. (Courtesy of Historic Photos Publishers.)

The champions of the 1912–1913 Sonoma-Napa-Solano Athletic League pictured here are, from left to right, (first row, kneeling) Victor Cole (who became a CPA and moved to Marin County), Elmer J. Salmina (who became a vintner), and Paul Alexander (who became a banker); (second row, standing) Lauren Mooney (who became an interior decorator living in Sausalito), Erwin Moore (who moved to Siskiyou County), and Louis D. Vasconi (who became an insurance agent and judge; see also page 65). (Courtesy of the St. Helena Historical Society.)

The 1933 men's basketball squad had good chances for the championship. Horace "Rip" Harrison, at over 6 feet in height, played center, and the running guard was Bill Wolf. Atilio "Toch" Ghiringhelli was good at sinking long shots. Pictured, from left to right, are (first row, kneeling) Bill Wolf, ? Mee, Art Merla, Harry Magnaghi, and unidentified; (second row, standing) Mac Salladay, Rip Harrison, Coach Loren Critser, Toch Ghiringhelli, and Marc Calleri. (Courtesy of Ida Merla Porterfield.)

This photograph shows the 1921 women's intramural basketball squad posing in their physical education uniforms. While the boys played other schools, the girls only played within the school. From left to right are (first row, kneeling) Bernell Palmer, Josephine Jackse, and Marie Zimmerman; (second row, standing) Doris Schroeder, Grace Walters, Betty Harrington, and Hazel Young. (Courtesy of Historic Photos Publishers.)

The women's baseball team, shown here with their coaches, is from the 1920s. Only two people have been identified, as follows: (first row, second from right) Antoinette Morosoli (Lynch) and (third row, second from right) Elmer J. Salmina, who was also a good basketball player. The two were cousins, whose families owned Larkmead Winery. (Courtesy of the St. Helena Historical Society.)

Preparing for graduation day in 1933 is Nemo Debely in his second year of teaching. He was born in Switzerland and came to the United States at age seven. Besides teaching chemistry, physics, and math, he was also the bandleader. A member of the University of California, Berkeley's gymnastic team, he gave annual tumbling shows for the students. He was a favorite teacher until his retirement in 1960. (Courtesy of Ida Merla Porterfield.)

Teacher Marietta Voorhees poses at a 1933 graduation ceremony in her third year as a high school teacher. She was known for her love of literature and for directing many plays. She resigned in protest in 1956 after the voters turned down a tax increase to fund raises in teachers' salaries. To fill her time, she opened a used bookstore in town, where she welcomed literature fans. (Courtesy of Ida Merla Porterfield.)

The Women's Improvement Club staged the annual May Day show for children in 1920. A skit written by Mary Signorelli had dancers gather in a large bowl surrounded by salad ingredients. From left to right are (first row) Mary Swift (sugar), Vera Light (red pepper), Dixie Chiles (lettuce), and Valma Bolster (the cook); (second row) Marie Zimmerman (vinegar), Hendrina Stewart (mustard), Mary Signorelli (salt), Margaret Chiles (tomato), and Vina Hinton (oil). (Courtesy of Historic Photos Publishers.)

Senior Sneak Day in 1924 took place on Mount St. Helena, where someone brought more than a camera! Sneakers, sitting from left to right, are (first row) Clinton March, John Rogers, unidentified, Fernand Vautier, Frank Harrison (see also pages 54 and 68), and Herbert Lutley. Standing from left to right are (second row) Abe Merowitz, W. W. "Jack" Lyman (see also page 82), Paul Herdle, William Thompson, and an unknown fellow partially hidden by William's arm. (Courtesy of the Frank and Edith Harrison Trust.)

Two lads, names unknown, grin cheekily at the camera as they share a drink, type also unknown, just before the end of Prohibition in 1933. (Courtesy of Ida Merla Porterfield.)

Mary Jane Twichell (left) and pal Eleanor Kayser sit on a friend's car just before high school graduation in 1933. Mary attended college, then married Delford Britton and mothered a large family. Her son, Delford "Del" Jr., is presently mayor of St. Helena. Eleanor came from a German family living in Rutherford. (Courtesy of Ida Merla Porterfield.)

Eight

OUTLYING AREAS

The Villa Hotel in Rutherford was constructed in 1883. As early as 1890, it was owned by Henry Hortop but managed for many years by his brother-in-law, William March, and his wife, May. Besides running the hotel, March was a longtime farmer. He was born in Missouri and moved to Suisun in 1925. (Courtesy of the George and Elsie Wood St. Helena Public Library.)

RUTHERFORD AVENUE, RUTHERFORD, NAPA CO., CAL.

Serranus Hastings donated the land to construct Rutherford Avenue east to the Napa River in 1867. By 1885, Rutherford had two large merchandise stores, Henry Hortop's carriage manufactory, the Villa Hotel, a livery stable, a lumberyard, a post office, a barley mill, and two saloons. Looking east down Rutherford Avenue in 1909, Hortop's Rutherford Agricultural Works and the department store are on the left. Hortop became known in the region for the manufacture and sale of carriages and farm equipment. (Courtesy of Jack and Marcey Smith).

The Rutherford store has a long history of different owners. In 1880, Joshua Frye ran the store, later taking on Frank Nottage as a partner. Henry Hortop bought the store in 1900 and sold it in 1909 to J. Jardine. This photograph was taken c. 1914, when Hartman and Klang operated it. Other owners included Morosoli, Bosetti, Caiocca and Tonella, Lightner and Ghiringhelli, Philo Grant, and Horace Onorato. Bill Giugni owned the establishment from 1955 to 1965. The building was demolished in 1971. (Courtesy of Jack and Marcey Smith.)

This 1917 photograph shows the White Rock Mine dump trucks lined up in Rutherford. Magnesite ore was transported from Pope Valley to Rutherford for crushing and shipment between 1906 and 1924. (Courtesy of the Harold Smith Sr. family.)

S. P. R. R. DEPOT, RUTHERFORD, NAPA CO., CAL.

The railroad came to Rutherford in 1868, making it a shipping point for grain from Pope and Chiles Valleys. This photograph shows Southern Pacific Engine 1478 making a stop in Rutherford around 1906. It was taken looking north, with the county road (now California State Route 29) on the right-hand side, just outside the picture. (Courtesy of Jack and Marcey Smith.)

When the railroad came to Oakville in 1868, H. W. Crabb sold land to build the depot, shown here prior to 1964. Crabb established the To-Kalon Wine Company in Oakville in 1872. Oakville consisted of a general store, a blacksmith shop, and a saloon in 1878. With the coming of the railroad, it became a shipping point for local farmers to send grain, fruit, and wine to market. The depot was destroyed by fire in 1964. (Courtesy of Jack and Marcey Smith.)

In 1906, a blacksmith shop called Lincoln and Hewitt was built at the corner of Oakville Cross Road and the county road (now California State Route 29). Ed Hewitt went into partnership with Alva and George Lincoln, teaching them about blacksmithing. By the late 1920s, automobiles had replaced wagons and horses, so the blacksmith shop became Lincoln Brothers Garage. The business moved to Rutherford in 1935 and later became Lincoln Tractor. (Courtesy of Bill and Barbara Lincoln.)

The Pope Valley Store was a center of activity for area residents for over a century. It served as a stopover for men traveling to the mines in Lake County. It was built about 1875, and in 1913, a second gable-roofed building was attached. The building housed a hotel, saloon, post office, and general store. Thomas L. G. Neil and Pauline Haug Neil moved to Pope Valley and became the owners in 1912. The photograph above was taken about 1914 and shows, from left to right, Elgy, Ralph, Tom, Roy, Pauline, and Leonora Neil. The photograph below shows the store in 1949. (Photographs courtesy of Joe Callizo.)

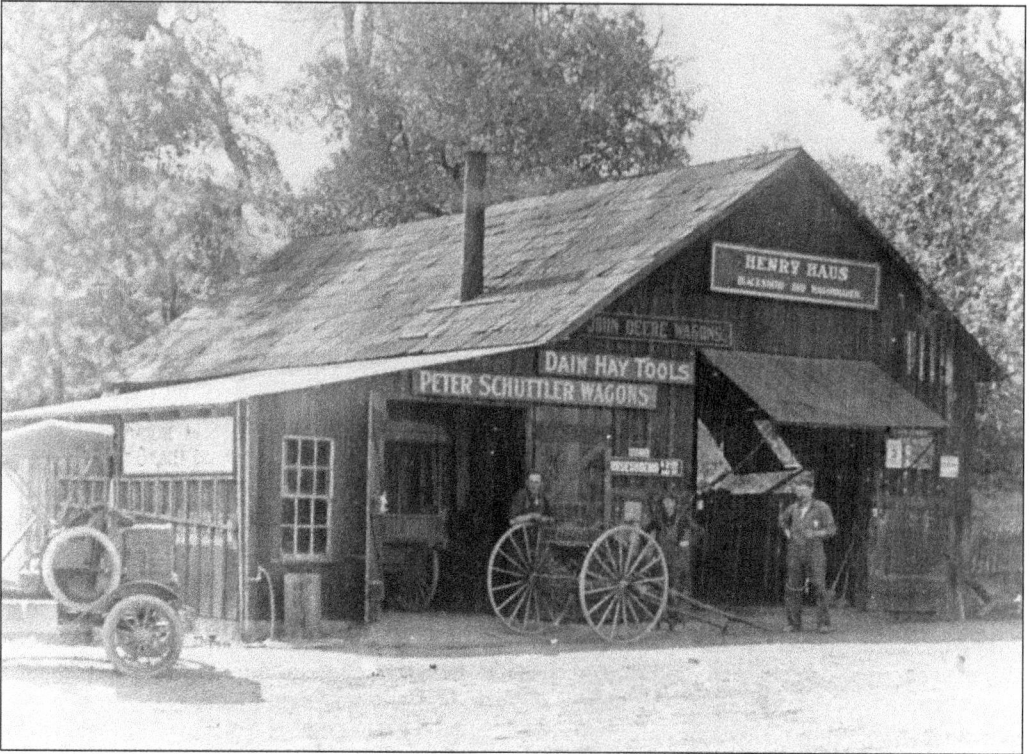

Henry Haus bought this blacksmith shop (shown above) in Pope Valley in 1898, where he shoed horses and repaired wagons. In 1952, when Henry retired, he locked the door and left everything as it was. In the photograph below, he relaxes with friends Lee Eakle, Pat Eakle, Spike the dog, and Elgie Rae Neil (Kirkpatrick). Today the Henry Haus Blacksmith Shop is one of the most historic farrieries in the country and is open by appointment with the Napa County Historical Society. (Photographs courtesy of Joe Callizo.)

The baseball diamond was located just behind the firehouse in Pope Valley in the 1920s. From left to right are (first row, on the ground) Elgy Neil, Roy Neil, Milton Young, Lawrence Groteguth, and Dudley Duvall; (second row, standing) Charlie Pfiester, Adolph Haug Jr., Edward Young, John Howe, Tommy Samuels, and Ted Hardin. (Courtesy of Joe Callizo.)

The Pope Valley Cornet Band poses in 1897. From left to right are (first row, kneeling or seated) Bill Harvey, Alec Clark, Herman Mast, Claude Duvall, Professor Barrat, Matt Mast, and Fred Mast; (second row, standing) Mark Hardin, Wade Thomas, Ernest Mast, Millie Overhulser, Lawrence J. Duvall, Grace Duvall, Jed Walters, John B. Duvall, Fannie Duvall, Henry Meyer, Laura Duvall, Gordon Stafford, Mallie Stafford, and Ed Young. (Courtesy of Joe Callizo.)

Napa County produced 40,000 tons of magnesite in 1917, when magnesium was required for the war effort. This is a southern view of the 11 White Rock Mine kilns located on Pope Canyon Road. Almost a million dollars' worth of magnesite was mined before the operation closed down in 1924. Before its vein of ore ran out, the mine was one of the most important sources of magnesium ore in California. (Courtesy of the Harold Smith Sr. family.)

The mine owner and his supervisors pose at the entrance to a tunnel at the White Rock Mine. From left to right, at the right of the photograph, the four men shown are Frank Sweasey (owner of the White Rock Mine from 1916 to 1921), Louis ?, Harold U. Smith (transport supervisor), and W. T. Lewis (superintendent). (Courtesy of the Harold Smith Sr. family.)

Harold Smith Sr. owned this fleet of trucks, employing 40 men to transport magnesite ore. The drivers drove ore over Howell Mountain to Rutherford for crushing and shipping by railroad. After mining ceased at White Rock Mine, Smith began a company that supplied gravel and cement, providing the materials for the construction of many roads in Napa County. (Courtesy of the Harold Smith Sr. family.)

"Seven trucks roared into our peaceful valley, loaded up with magnesite, and started to the nearest railroad. Their path was blocked by a mountain with muddy roads and each one was in up to their hubs. The drivers abandoned them for several days until the roads were drier." It was a bad time for White Rock Mine trucks to attempt the trip to Rutherford, and they got stuck in Angwin on February 16, 1921. (Courtesy of the Harold Smith Sr. family.)

Aetna Springs opened its doors in 1873 to become a popular resort for prosperous city dwellers to swim, hike, fish, and golf. "Aetna Springs are widely known as having waters possessing highly medicinal qualities and are curative for many diseases." Travelers came by train to Calistoga and over the rough Oat Hill Mine Road, but later took the train to St. Helena and the stage over Howell Mountain Road. By 1906, Len Owens owned the springs and began renovations, making it one of the most popular vacation spots in the state. Above, Owens rides in a car leaving Aetna Springs in about 1910. He retired in 1945 and sold the resort to George and Ruth Heibel, whose family helped pamper the guests. Resort guests dressed up for dinner each evening, as seen below in the dining room in the late 1940s. (Photographs courtesy of Joe Callizo.)

The McCormick ranch was settled in 1844 by William McCormick and Molly Hudson McCormick. It comprised about 3,000 acres at the top of Spring Mountain near St. Helena, and sheep were raised there. Their son, John, eventually took over the ranch; he also served as county supervisor and was active in the Napa County Farm Bureau. When he married Ethel Roseberry in 1911, pal Jake Beringer was his best man. The couple had two daughters, Ina McCormick (Hart) and Babe McCormick (Learned). In the photograph above, John handles the reins on a Sunday drive. Below, his sister, Arlene McCormick, sits with an unidentified Native American woman and a family member around 1890. (Photographs courtesy of the St. Helena Historical Society.)

In 1877, Edwin Angwin's Howell Mountain Retreat, located in a small valley east of St. Helena, quickly became a popular resort. Edwin added to his land holdings until he had 1,500 acres. He sold the property to Pacific Union College in 1909. The resort's hotel, bowling alleys, and cottages became dormitories, classrooms, and faculty homes. (Courtesy of the Clyde Kirkpatrick Collection.)

The Rural Health Retreat opened in 1878 with a two-story building, adding three more stories in 1890. It was designed to care for the whole person—body, mind, and spirit—through natural means. The name was changed to the St. Helena Sanitarium in 1898. A stagecoach drove to the St. Helena train station to pick up guests. The first mechanical transportation making it up the steep hill to the sanitarium was called a Doble steam car, shown here. (Courtesy of Jack and Marcey Smith.)

A big celebration took place at the Metzner farm in Conn Valley in 1891. From left to right are (front left) Frederick, Walter, and Arnold Metzner; (front right) Elise Metzner, Rosa Trumpler Metzner; and (standing) Louis Metzner. Frederick, a Swiss immigrant, was a partner in the Franco-Swiss Winery with Germain Crochat. Walter became the pharmacist and owner of Smith's Pharmacy and mayor of St. Helena (see also pages 43, 53, and 70). Arnold worked for Shell Oil and in real estate. Louis became a butcher and partner in Knox Meat Market. (Courtesy of Gail Morgan Lane.)

Lola Cowan and Eleanore Mayers ride their horses to school in Conn Valley around 1917. Their teacher, Frances Korte (Pagendarm), snapped a photograph of these eighth graders, who were about to graduate. (Courtesy of the Korte Family Collection.)

Prune Inspecting

Two Brothers – Clem & Ben Korte

Clemens and Bernard Korte were born in Germany in the 1860s and came to America in 1887. Clemens settled on Ehlers Lane at a ranch still owned by the Korte family. Bernard bought property in Calistoga and became a farmer. Here the brothers inspect the prune crop at the Ehlers Lane ranch, where they also had a vineyard. (See also 11, 12, 14, 16, and 91.) (Courtesy of the Korte Family Collection.)

Hops are important to the beer-making process. Here harvesters stuff hops into sacks for drying in the hop barn. St. Helena's prize-winning hops were grown by five producers: Cole and Simpson, Storey Brothers, James Dowdell, R. F. Lane, and Phillip Elting. In 1884, the whole crop was 115 tons. Edward Fautz probably bought local hops for his St. Helena Brewery. (Courtesy of the St. Helena Historical Society.)

The Bale Mill, built in 1846 by Dr. Edward Turner Bale, was one of the earliest structures in upper Napa Valley, and it is restored and operating today as a state park. Marie Stabo (upper right corner) poses with a square dance group at the Bale Mill around 1955. The little girl in front is Dona Stanley. Her grandparents, Charles and Bernice Stanley, were caretakers of the mill at the time. (Courtesy of the St. Helena Historical Society.)

At Aetna Springs Resort in 1965, George Heibel introduced Ronald Reagan at a meeting of the Napa County Republicans, with over 500 in attendance. While exploring a run for governor, Reagan gave a rousing political speech on the issues facing California. Wallace Everett, congressman Don Clausen, and state senator John McCarthy also spoke. Here Reagan poses with Heibel, Starr Baldwin (editor of the local newspaper; see also page 60), and Helen Heibel (Nelson) while in the buffet line. (Courtesy of Helen Heibel Nelson.)

Visit us at
arcadiapublishing.com